THE ILLUSIONS OF REALITY

TROMPE-L'ŒIL PAINTING

THE ILLUSIONS OF REALITY

TROMPE-L'ŒIL PAINTING

by Miriam Milman
D.Phil. (Oxon.)

SKIRA
RIZZOLI

©1982 by Editions d'Art Albert Skira S.A., Geneva

Reproduction rights reserved by A.D.A.G.P. and
S.P.A.D.E.M., Paris, and Cosmopress, Geneva

Published in the United States of America in 1983 by
RIZZOLI INTERNATIONAL PUBLICATIONS, INC.
712 Fifth Avenue/New York 10019

Library of Congress Catalog Card Number: 82-42851

ISBN: 0-8478-0470-4

Printed in Switzerland

Foreword

"Zeuxis... uvas pictas tanto successu ut in scaenam aves advolarent." [1] A study of trompe-l'œil inevitably begins with Pliny's story of Zeuxis and the birds who took his painted grapes for real ones. Zeuxis himself was taken in when he tried to draw the curtain painted by his rival Parrhasius. But that is not the whole of the story. When Zeuxis painted a boy carrying some grapes and the birds came again to peck at the fruit, he considered that he had failed: the grapes had drawn the birds, but the boy had not been painted convincingly enough to frighten the birds away.

In front of a painting or sculpture the spectator is in fact continually being deceived. Stone has to suggest life; a fixed image has to convey an action or a mood; a canvas or a wall, two-dimensional surfaces, have to suggest space, which has three dimensions. As in the story of Zeuxis, this deception is more or less successful. It is also, over the centuries, more or less deliberate; it often requires of the spectator a certain complicity. It is by delimiting its extent that we can define what is meant by realism, illusionism, and lastly trompe-l'œil.

In the realm of creative art scholastic definitions are not very useful. Here, however, it seems necessary to be explicit about some of the terms which, otherwise, are apt to be confusing. [2]

In this book the term *realistic* applies only to the *rendering* of the work; that is, to the textural quality of the objects detached from their context, and not to the work as a whole, nor to its content. When a sufficient number of details are treated realistically, the artist has complied with only part of the conditions necessary to create an *illusionistic* work.

An essential factor in obtaining the illusion of truth is the way the painter conveys the sense of *space*. Here we touch on the problem of perspective, of the whole body of empirical or mathematical methods employed to give a two-dimensional picture the semblance of that third dimension which is essential to the world around us.

Finally, it must not be forgotten that in front of a picture, however illusionistic it may be, the spectator has to exercise his will in order to enter this fictive world, sharply cut off by a frame or wall. The entry into it has become instantaneous and almost unconscious for the Westerner, who is surrounded by pictures and accustomed and educated to consider them as fictions conveying the illusion of a certain reality. [3] Once he has entered the world of the picture, the spectator finds himself in a context whose *content* may strike him as more or less truthful. [4] The reality of a sacred vision or a mythological legend is the result of an act of faith. On the other hand, the so-called genre scene may be made more credible by the familiarity of the subject.

To enter the pictured world, then, an act of volition is called for. Having accepted the content as possible, one is led also, by the realism of details and the construction of space, to accept the *illusion* of the reality conjured up by the whole.

With the trompe-l'œil picture, on the other hand, the experience is carried through to the end. The spectator does not have to take the first step of accepting the work as a *representation*. He is surprised and deceived at the first sight of it. His eyes tell him that what he sees here is an integral part of his familiar visual world, and his reaction is not to accept what he knows is only an illusion, but to test its reality by reaching out and touching it. The mystification is complete. It is deliberately sought by the artist,[5] who is playing a game with his viewers. This game, like any game, if it is to be successful, has to obey certain rules, which we may now analyse.

Trompe-l'œil has to create this initial impression of surprise—more or less momentary before the spectator realizes the hoax. Obviously, if it is to transcend the game and also interest a spectator of taste and knowledge, trompe-l'œil has to offer something deeper, it has to convey a message or establish a dialogue. If this second act of the encounter fails to take place, then the trompe-l'œil remains a hoax, a procedure, a meaningless décor. It has often been dismissed as such.

The *illusion* of reality gives the artist a margin of freedom, since the spectator is prepared to accept the imaginary world brought before him. One might say, in the language of modern mathematics, that illusionistic painting as a set is implicitly larger and that it *contains* the sub-set of trompe-l'œil. Trompe-l'œil derives from the experience of the illusionism of which it is one of the outcomes.

It seemed interesting and necessary to study some of the works—referred to in the literature as both *illusionist* and *trompe-l'œil*—which show clearly enough that the artist's intention was to create a world acceptable as a reality. As we consider the realistic modelling, the eye-deceiving detail and the illusionistic procedures, we shall try to point out where the artist succeeds and where he fails, and so gradually establish the criteria of what makes a trompe-l'œil painting.

Realistic rendering and trompe-l'œil detail

It is extremely difficult to put into words the qualities of the painter's handling which convey the almost tactile sense of reality. The words *relief, modelling, chiaroscuro*, are part of the vocabulary of all illusionist painting. Instead of defining each of these qualities and looking at the ways they apply, it seems more rewarding to discuss several eloquent examples of them.

When one speaks of the *realistic texture* of a picture, one thinks inevitably of the Flemish masters of the fifteenth century. They were the first to achieve this quality of absolute reality in the rendering of detail. Take the *Annunciation* of Rogier van der Weyden: the objects, while charged with their symbolic meaning, [1] nevertheless stand out from the context of the image by the sheer force of their pictorial presence. Following in the tradition of Van Eyck, the painter contrives to render the specific tangibility of matter, to an almost microscopic degree.

The miniature of the Master of Mary of Burgundy is a brilliant demonstration of the range of modulations which Flemish art of the fifteenth century had at its command. The cushion, book and jewelry are the personal belongings of Mary of Burgundy who, having just left the room, has given up her place to the spectator. The latter is invited to read the pages of her prayer book; looking up through the opening in the wall, he will have, as she has just had, a vision of Christ being nailed to the Cross. The picture is thus seen to extend over three levels of reality, to embody three ways of conveying a speaking image. In the foreground, the real world of objects; beyond that, the visionary world of the Passion scene, deliberately drained of reality, which seems to merge into the mists of the imaginary. Finally, the artist skilfully contrives to introduce a third level of *non-reality*: the image of the Crucifixion in the open book which, roughly sketched out and faintly coloured, is not a vision but an illustration.

Rogier van der Weyden (1399-1464):
The Annunciation, entire and detail,
c. 1435. Oil on panel.

Other works, while never quite managing to deceive the spectator, must also be seen as reflecting the same intention. Such are the niches containing pottery, [2] as well as the flowers and animals that cast their shadow in the margins of illuminated manuscripts of the School of Bruges. In all these works the realism of the pictorial rendering is carefully calculated to establish the degree of reality of the scene.

It was also in the fifteenth century that certain details appeared which reveal the artist's intention of introducing elements fraught with a more aggressive reality than the rest of the picture. As evidence of Giotto's precocity, the story goes that, as a joke, while still an apprentice in Cimabue's workshop, he painted a fly on the nose of a figure so convincingly that the master was taken in and tried to chase it away. The story is apocryphal, and flies only made their appearance in painting a hundred years later, both in the North and in Italy. [3]

Master of Mary of Burgundy (15th century):

Page from the Prayer Book of Engelbert of Nassau: The Procession of the Kings, c. 1485-1490. Painting on vellum.

◁ Page from the Prayer Book of Mary of Burgundy, before 1477. Painting on vellum.

As regards the life-size fly that figures in the wedding portrait of the Master of Frankfurt or the one attracting the attention of Carlo Crivelli's Virgin and Child, it seems unlikely that they are a token of the painter's sense of humour. Here already they may be charged with that symbolism of death and decay which they convey in the Vanitas pictures of the years to come. At about the same period the *cartellino* makes its appearance—a small slip of paper skilfully folded, with its edges turned down and bearing the painter's signature or other inscriptions. As a luminous surface, its whiteness immediately visible, the *cartellino* stands out from the picture and enters unequivocally the world of the spectator. It also brings a direct message from the artist to the public. The signature, date or title [4] inscribed on the *cartellino* go to establish it as a *real* object, while thrusting the picture content back into the world of illusion. The folded or crumpled scrap of paper standing out so effectively from the plane surface of the painted picture later became a stock device of trompe-l'œil painting. [5] Likewise, the feet slipping over the edge of the earliest miniatures and the hands protruding from the frame of portraits are trompe-l'œil details which painters have resorted to throughout the centuries for the purpose of linking up their pictures with the reality of the spectator.

△ Jacob Cornelisz van Oostsanen,
called Jacob van Amsterdam (c. 1470-1533):
Self-Portrait, 1533.
Oil on panel.

◁ Carlo Crivelli (1430-1493):
Madonna and Child.
Tempera and gold on panel.

▷ Master of Frankfurt (late 15th-early 16th century):
Portrait of the Artist and his Wife,
1480. Oil on panel.

2

The conquest
of the
third dimension

The study of the Pompeian frescoes shows clearly that, even in ancient times, artists who set out to paint a cycle of pictures giving the illusion of reality have tried to overcome the flat surface of the wall. They did so in two ways.

In some cases they did away with the background wall by opening up a new space which extended that of the spectator by increasing its depth. Here we have an *evasion* beyond the barrier plane.

In other cases the background wall is left in place, and the third dimension is obtained through the *invasion* of the spectator's space by the picture space. The painted scene is projected out of its frame and seems to enter the real world. There are of course examples in which both solutions are found side by side.

evasion:

abolition of the wall

In Roman wall painting of the Second Style the wall is often made to disappear and give place to garden vistas and architectural perspectives. The perspective system at that time (in so far as one may speak of a coherent perspective [1]) was not based on a single viewpoint, so that without too much contradiction it allowed for the mobility of the spectator. What might have been a flaw in the optics of the *costruzione legittima* here promotes the effect of illusion.

That the Pompeian wall paintings were designed as purely illusionist decorations is clear from the fact that in several houses the viewpoint from which they can be best appreciated is marked on the floor. The spectator's complicity is solicited and his reaction conditioned before he even sees the work, thus eliminating the element of surprise essential to one's initial contact with a trompe-l'œil. [2]

The artist who, with so much refinement, decorated the patrician villa of Oplontis seems to have understood perfectly the limits of his art, giving prominence to a foreground of fluted columns which thrust the wall back slightly. The latter opens up at the back to disclose an elegant, well-lit building with two rows of superimposed colonnades. While the simulated

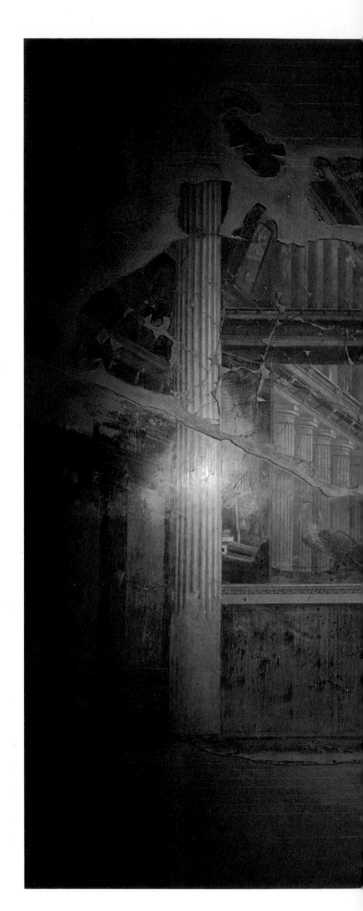

Roman Villa at Oplontis near Naples:
Fresco Painting
of the mid-first century B.C.

Castello di Issogne in the Val d'Aosta:
Fresco in the Sala Baronale,
15th century.

▷Baldassare Peruzzi (1481-1536):
Fresco in the Hall of Columns
of the Villa Farnesina, Rome, c. 1515.

interior architecture seems to envelop the spectator on three sides, the external building at the back merges with the sky in a rapid aerial perspective, with a skilful harmony of colours. The easel pictures, inclined and framed,[3] are placed on the upper beams. Everything seems to have been known already to these painters of some two thousand years ago.

In the fifteenth-century wall paintings in the Baronial Hall of the Castle of Issogne, the spectator's space is separated from the panoramic landscape by simulated columns in transparent rock crystal or veined marble alternating with fine brocades. The landscape combines in one vision the real world of neighbouring castles perched on crags in the Val d'Aosta with the biblical world of Golgotha and the Holy City of Jerusalem. The opulent presence of the columns comes as a challenge to the intricate perspective constructions, for in this context the columns do not require any privileged viewpoint in order to convey the tactile sense of their roundness and impose their

reality. Using the technique of a Flemish miniaturist, this unknown artist has produced a fresco which almost compels the eye to accept the reality of the scene represented.

In the Hall of Columns of the Villa Farnesina, on the other hand, Baldassare Peruzzi makes full use of the knowledge gained by Renaissance theorists. With unfailing virtuosity he joins up the simulated architecture with the actual walls by means of painted columns, thus integrating it into the apparent thickness of the wall. Thanks to this recession, the artist has introduced a loggia opening on a panoramic view of Rome.

This fresco apparently possesses all the qualities required of a trompe-l'œil, but it has the weakness inherent in flawless and spectacular perspectives—namely, that these are legible only from a mathematically defined point. Everything is constructed for a spectator, and for one only, provided that he is motionless.[4]

Giovanni Battista Albanese
(first half of the 17th century):
Drawing of the Proscenium of
Palladio's Teatro Olimpico, Vicenza.
Pen and watercolour.

Andrea Mantegna (1431-1506):
Ceiling Fresco in the Camera degli Sposi,
◁ Palazzo Ducale, Mantua, 1461-1474.

In order to recreate the space and structure of Roman buildings, Andrea Mantegna *opened up* the vault of the Camera degli Sposi, in the Ducal Palace at Mantua, and let the sky show through. The artists of previous centuries had already painted church vaults blue and dotted them with stars in order to evoke the Celestial World. But with Mantegna the innovation also consists in placing life-size figures in period costumes on the balcony circling round the opening. In Mantegna this piercing of the vault is seen as an evasion towards the sky, for apart from the putti the figures are kept behind the railing and do not invade the viewer's space. Later the opening up of the vault goes almost unnoticed because of the heavenly hosts filling it up as they burst into the world of reality. The architectural background opening up a deep recession into external space is a constant feature of sixteenth-century painting, and the fascination it exerted accounts for its use in various forms for several generations to come. [5] It may have originated in the interest aroused by the laws of perspective and in the admiration felt for the sober buildings and spacious squares of antiquity. The painted architecture of Francesco di Giorgio Martini and Sangallo brings us to the stage setting, of which we have a rare and spectacular example in that of Palladio at Vicenza. For it was in the theatre that the painted architectural perspective approached most nearly to trompe-l'œil. Its success was due not only to the quality of the work, but also to the circumstances of its use, which immobilized the spectator and gave life to the scenes enacted between himself and the setting.

the wall thrust back

Mural painting has often abolished the wall by thrusting it back and disclosing some other self-contained space. The painters of Pompeii repeatedly used this procedure, as can be seen in the Villa of Lucrezio Frontone or the House of the Gladiators. These niches (or spaces closed off at the back) contain objects or statues, sometimes also what appear to be easel paintings.

In the Scrovegni Chapel in Padua, Giotto *pierced* the wall of the triumphal arch with two *coretti* from which lanterns hang and which give a view on to the *secret chapels*. It is quite possible that these surprising representations, executed in a coherent converging perspective, were meant to simulate the existence of a transept which was planned but never built. [6] It is also probable that for the spectator seated during the divine service, and therefore motionless, the *coretti* constituted a real trompe-l'œil created in another spirit, with a different intention from that which governed the body of frescoes in the chapel.

As in Roman basilicas, the dado of Early Christian and Romanesque churches was decorated with draperies and marbles painted in trompe-l'œil. Charles de Tolnay [7] has drawn attention to the survival of several twelfth-century examples in Tuscany—of actual niches built into this lower zone, their back wall being painted to represent the liturgical objects which they contained. The real object was thus placed in front of its image, which here played the part of a topographical indication.

This idea evolved, and in Santa Croce in Florence (Taddeo Gaddi) and in the Lower Church of San Francesco at Assisi (Lorenzetti) we find false niches entirely painted. [8] Figuring on the dado of the chapels, they have no iconographical connection with the narrative frescoes above them. These images are painted in the very place where the cult objects which they represent should have been located, in the real niches which these images simulate. [9] They are executed in an advanced technique for the period, vigorously emphasizing relief and transparency by a skilful play of light and shade. So successful are these initial evocations of the volume of an object and the space it occupies, so intent is the artist on building up a composition, that far from being a mere decorative feat [10] these painted niches compel recognition as the incunabula of still life painting. The fact that they are successful pieces of trompe-l'œil only adds to their interest.

One responds more immediately to the ludic aspect taken on by the self-portrait of Paolo Schiavo drawing aside the curtain of a simulated niche painted under the frescoes in the Collegiate church of

Taddeo Gaddi (?-1366):
Niche with Cruets in the
Baroncelli Chapel, Church of
Santa Croce, Florence. Fresco.

◁ Giotto (1266-1337):
Coretto on the wall of the Triumphal Arch,
Cappella degli Scrovegni, Padua,
1305. Fresco.

Paolo Schiavo (1397-1478):
Self-Portrait in the Collegiate
Church of Castiglione Olona (Lombardy).
Fresco.

▷ Paolo Antonio Brunetti (1723-1783):
Decoration in the Chapelle des Ames du
Purgatoire, Church of Sainte-Marguerite,
Paris, 1764.

Castiglione Olona.[11] Half concealed by the altar, the
painter contemplates his work and the congregation,
thus setting up a dialogue with the spectator who, if
not deceived, is certainly surprised by this unexpected
presence. One of the earliest independent self-
portraits on record,[12] this face in trompe-l'œil asserts
itself much more boldly than those of other artists
disguised as secondary figures among the heroes of
their frescoes.

False niches were an important element in the mural
decoration of palaces and churches. They were
usually ˌpeopled with statues in grisaille, perfect
imitations of the marble which they replaced. The
style of such works may be sober and austere; such is
the case with the frescoes in grisaille in the chapel
painted by Brunetti in the Paris church of Sainte-
Marguerite. But in the princely villas and palaces of
Italy, France and England, from the sixteenth to the
eighteenth century, we usually find an atmosphere of
ostentation and exuberance which leads to the
extension of the festivities to the imaginary architectural space beyond the barrier of the wall.

Paolo Veronese (1528-1588):
Fresco in the Stanza dell'Olimpo,
Villa Barbaro, Maser (Venetia),
c. 1560.

Such is the spirit that prevails in the villas decorated by Veronese and Tiepolo, where the coloured statues stand out from their niches, the doors open towards shadowy spaces, and monumental staircases lead up to non-existing balconies. These frescoes, like Mantegna's, are usually peopled with life-size figures in the costumes of the period. The mirror play of reflected figures in the room, meeting with their double (sometimes with their own portrait) in the narrow opening of a door, at the top of a staircase or on a balcony, creates a pervasive ambiguity which is characteristic of trompe-l'œil, only flawed here by their immobility.

Following a strangely similar line of approach, some four centuries later, Michelangelo Pistoletto replaces the wall and its fresco with a polished steel mirror on which is cast the moving, reflected image of the viewer. The latter becomes the protagonist of a game watched by the painted paper-cut silhouettes seen in back view. As in Veronese, a balcony—a barrier—separates the actors and spectators. Pistoletto thus achieves the eye-deceiving illusion of an unreal world, one where the roles are reversed, where virtual images blend with reality in a baffling confusion.

Michelangelo Pistoletto (1933):
Woman and Nurse, 1967.
Cut-out photograph painted over
and pasted on polished steel.

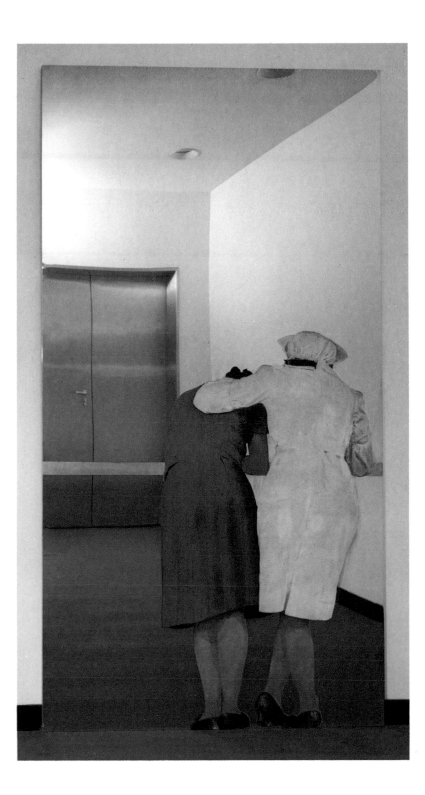

invasion: the elements of architecture

For reasons of economy perhaps, but certainly for *illusionistic* reasons too, painters have invaded the world of the spectator with simulated architecture, tapestries, statues and bas-reliefs.

Again the Pompeii wall paintings vouch for the antiquity of this procedure, and it was by no means forgotten in the Middle Ages. A close study of the interior of the Florentine Baptistery (thirteenth century) shows the boldness of the complex architectural structure suggested by the decoration. [13]

Quadratura [14] has always been an effective means of creating the illusion of the third dimension, and simulated architectural elements projecting outwards have been a constant feature of mural decoration. [15] So long as their depth does not exceed that of the pilasters (that is, so long as they remain attached to the wall), such elements have been successful as a trompe-l'œil device. But when the simulated architecture assumes the proportion of columns and instead of a *setting* becomes the principal feature, when these columns collapse and invade the spectator's space, [16] then the fiction exceeds the limits of credibility. Furthermore, no element *in motion* can act as a trompe-l'œil.

As we have seen in the section dealing with *evasion*, the construction of deeply receding spaces creates a feeling of tension for the spectator as soon as he moves away from the perspective viewpoint. This stress becomes noticeably unpleasant when the architecture seen "di sotto in su" extends vertically and advances towards the spectator. The sense of distortion is accompanied by an impression of instability, by a feeling that the whole building is about to collapse. When Baroque artists like Andrea Pozzo and Antonio Verrio proceed to invade the spectator's space with buildings and heavenly hosts, all pretence of illusion disappears and the effect becomes almost ludicrous.

Andrea Pozzo (1642-1709):
Glory of St Francis Xavier
in the Chiesa del Gesù, Mondovì
(Piedmont), 1670. Fresco.

Baldassare Croce (c. 1558-1628):
Susanna and the Elders.
Church of Santa Susanna, Rome.
Fresco.

simulated tapestry

Already known in antiquity, simulated draperies were used as a decorative element in the lower parts of Early Christian churches. Like any representation of reality *at a second remove*, the representation of tapestries may be a successful and easily achieved trompe-l'œil device. It is one that gives the artist complete freedom; any subject is acceptable, since it is relegated to the totally unreal world represented by the tapestry.

The artist is free to paint his simulated tapestry without any of the constraint imposed by perspective, since it is meant to have no depth and the tucked-up folds or edges, together with the hangings over a doorway, offer a particularly effective means of suggesting the tactile reality of a fabric.

Simulated tapestries were frequently represented in the sixteenth and seventeenth centuries. Combined with trompe-l'œil statuary and architecture, they emphasize the ambiguity of the decorative system employed in Mannerist and Baroque painting. [17]

simulated sculpture

The painters of Pompeii, Giotto in the Scrovegni Chapel in Padua, the School of Raphael in the Vatican Stanze, all represented false statues, in imitation marble, which are not set back in niches but seem to stand out from the wall. Like imitation bas-reliefs in grisaille, these works were first used as secondary decorative motifs in rooms adorned with illusionist frescoes.

Thus, for the Stanza di Eliodoro, Raphael designed [18] a monochrome decoration animated by caryatids and terms which seem to support the frescoed wall.

Though set within a recess, the caryatid standing under the fresco of *St Peter Delivered from Prison by an Angel* has one arm which passes in front of the cornice, while the other pierces the spectator's space with a resolute gesture.

Salient reliefs gained in prominence with respect to figural scenes when designed to imitate stuccoes and blend with them in the painted decoration of the School of Fontainebleau palaces, and it is the equivocal presence of such reliefs which imparts their originality to the frescoes of Annibale Carracci. During the seventeenth and eighteenth centuries, simulated reliefs were a prominent feature of the decorative paintings in churches, in princely residences, and in the temporary constructions erected for royal ceremonies. [19]

Annibale Carracci (1560-1609):
Diana and Endymion in the Main
Gallery of the Palazzo Farnese, Rome,
1597-1604. Fresco.

painted facades

After antiquity and the Middle Ages which decorated their façades with geometric designs, Venice and Tuscany introduced a continuous tradition of façades adorned with grisailles.[20] But it is in Rome, in the early sixteenth century, that we find the greatest profusion of external decorations. These façades painted in trompe-l'œil, representing niches containing a statue or friezes in salient relief, were the work of artists keenly interested in archaeology, like Baldassare Peruzzi and Polidoro da Caravaggio. They thus catered for the pressing demands of a Tuscan nouveaux riches clientele who had come to Rome in successive waves, in the entourage of the popes. Rome at that time found itself transformed into a "great triumphal machine,"[21] a sumptuous but shortlived display of stage scenery.

While the painters of the past accepted the invading wall and ennobled it, those of the twentieth century (sometimes anonymous) seek above all to do away with it. So that the trompe-l'œil façades of today usually come as a cry of revolt against the wall that offends, that one would like to conjure away and forget, against the inhuman city that one is intent on escaping from.

Fabio Rieti (1925):
"Bach," at the corner of
rue Clisson-rue Jean-Sébastien Bach,
Paris. Painted façade.

overcoming the wall surface: achievement or failure?

In the foregoing pages we have looked at a few examples of illusionistic wall painting which suggest particularly well the three-dimensional space. But do they also succeed in taking in the spectator? What about the results of their success and the lessons of their failure? By its very nature, wall painting had the advantage of its scale, answering to the measure of nature and man, and also of the spectacular use it could make of perspective, which was devised for the express purpose of simulating the third dimension of the actual world.

In practically all the examples considered, the virtuosity of the perspective runs counter to the veracity of the trompe-l'œil. And the reason is that it requires the spectator to remain motionless at the particular point of vantage. Only when the depth of the field represented was minimal could the painted picture be accepted as a substitute for reality.

The presence of living figures caught in frozen attitudes very soon dispels the trompe-l'œil effect. The sense of reality is all the more ephemeral for today's viewer because for him these figures evoke no more than the ghosts of the past.

Where, on the other hand, the trompe-l'œil effect is markedly successful is in the use of the shallow niche and the architectural detail in low relief.

The representation in painting of another work of art, whether tapestry or monochrome statuary, opens up a limitless field of subjects for trompe-l'œil.

Warren Johnson:
"Tunnel Vision," 1975, Columbia, South
Carolina. Painted façade of a bank.

3

Trompe-l'œil and easel painting

The requirements as to the qualities of trompe-l'œil wall painting immediately limit the repertory of the easel works to be considered.

The need for life-size representation and the unconvincing nature of portrayals of living beings rule out the whole corpus of religious or mythological scenes, as well as portraits and landscapes. On the other hand, any subject can be given trompe-l'œil treatment as long as it is consigned to a second level of representation, in other words if it is presented as a trompe-l'œil.

We are left with what seems on the face of it to be the ideal field of still life. Is any still life treated in a realistic manner a trompe-l'œil? As in the case of wall painting, analysing one or two still lifes will enable us to define the requirements of trompe-l'œil more precisely.

Georg Flegel's *Still Life with Rummer, Pretzels and Almonds* treats its subject with startling veracity. Each element is charged with religious symbolism, and the skilful composition, culminating in a pyramid with the curve of the pretzel, might to the purist's eye look somewhat artificial. The dark, indeterminate background obscures all the problems posed by depth perspective. Yet not for one moment do we feel that we are in front of something real. This is partly due to the fact that the scale employed magnifies everything in such a way that the whole gives the impression of being viewed from above as through a lens. And lastly the way in which the table is cut off by the edge of the painting sharply draws attention to the limits of the pictorial field. The setting is not true to life. Even had there been no frame separating the painting from its surroundings, the objects contained in it would have had to be present in their entirety and the spectator's eye should not have had to look for the continuation of the table beyond the painting's edge. Flegel's work may be a realistic *still life*, but it is certainly not a trompe-l'œil.

The *Flower Piece in a Niche* by Ambrosius Bosschaert has a perfectly coherent setting for a trompe-l'œil, and we can imagine it being presented on a wall in which such an aperture might logically have figured. But the way in which the artist has constructed the bunch of flowers and the graphic treatment of the flowers themselves both derive from a tradition [1] that has nothing to do with the faithful representation of reality and even less with tactile suggestion of it.

This picture raises the problem of the presence of flowers in a trompe-l'œil. Even if they are not actually *alive*, painting gives them a stiffness they do not possess. And while artists have managed to "deceive the eye" when depicting inanimate objects, they have been less successful when depicting flowers.

Bosschaert's still life raises the further problem of a landscape being present in the background of a trompe-l'œil painting. It is clear from this work that *aerial* perspective, with its very high viewpoint, its gradual range of colours, and its bluish horizons, is in fact no more than an interpretation giving a feeling of distance without the certainty of it.

We are led to the conclusion that, if there are good reasons why an easel trompe-l'œil should be a still life, not every still life executed in a realistic manner is necessarily a trompe-l'œil.

Ambrosius Bosschaert (1573-1621):
Flower Piece in a Niche, c. 1620.
Oil on panel.

◁ Georg Flegel (1566-1638):
Still Life with Rummer,
Pretzels and Almonds, 1637.
Oil on panel.

Our analysis of the illusionism created by certain wall paintings as well as of the limited verisimilitude of still lifes has brought us to the point where we can define more precisely the rules artists must follow if they are to meet the *sine qua non* conditions of trompe-l'œil. Our list may appear pragmatic and inappropriate to the creation of a work of art. Indeed it is because of these restrictions that questions will inevitably arise concerning the artistic value of trompe-l'œil painting. In employing a necessarily limited vocabulary, this type of pictorial work is poised dangerously between the artefact on the one hand and the work of art on the other. For the same reason trompe-l'œil has often been relegated en bloc to the level of *decoration* or the visual *gag*. Yet the restrictions are real ones and, even if they have detracted from the richness of the repertory and from the prestige of trompe-l'œil painting, awareness and acceptance of them are essential to the process of creation and reception.

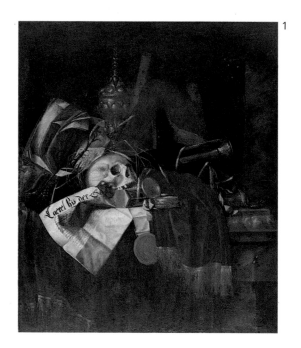

the rules of the game

1. A trompe-l'œil must be life-size.
2. It must fit perfectly in the setting in which it is presented, which means that its position and framing must both be logical. Taking this argument to its conclusion, we have to face the fact that the trompe-l'œil may suffer from presentation in a museum, for its proper place is there where the object (or objects) that it replaces should have been.
3. No element represented in the painting must be cut off by the edge of the painted surface.
4. The breakthrough into the third dimension must not be achieved by means of too deep or too protrusive a perspective system. [2] Perfect, dramatic *costruzione legittima* is detrimental to trompe-l'œil because the semblance of reality is removed by the slightest movement on the part of the spectator. The compromise provided by certain less rigorous types of construction allows a certain freedom of vision. For the same reasons it is clear that the feeling of depth and relief must be achieved by other means. *Invasion* of the spectator's space is more likely to be successful than *evasion* from it and is best achieved by laying thin elements one on top of another.
5. Relief and volume will be crucially dependent on the technique employed, the roots of which go back to the realistic rendering of fifteenth-century Flemish painting. Oil and coloured varnishes will be the most effective media because they enable the artist to make his brushstrokes invisible, blend his colours, and impart the requisite brilliance.
"More real than reality" is often the effect to be aimed at, [3] and hard outlines, dark shadows, and cut-away shapes all form part of the vocabulary of trompe-l'œil.
6. Live figures are to be avoided. Their frozen appearance commands little belief in their reality, and they become mere objects. Moreover, unlike objects, they date very quickly.

Obviously this list of restrictive conditions is the outcome of *a posteriori* analysis [4] of the material. But no discussion of trompe-l'œil is possible unless its sphere of existence and its limits are clearly defined. These *rules of the game* have imposed themselves on the painter and govern his composition and his technique. They also suggest almost implicitly the typology of trompe-l'œil painting. Within this rigid framework, the iconography of the image has changed over the centuries in line with the reality that the trompe-l'œil painting is regarded as replacing.

The three Gijsbrechts paintings all illustrate the Vanitas theme. Artist and subject are thus the same, and a similar vocabulary of symbolic objects is depicted. Yet these works are subtly different on a level other than that of their pictorial composition. Simply becoming aware of the levels of reality represented by these pictures makes the contact with each one of them more enriching.

Cornelis Norbertus Gijsbrechts
(c. 1610-after 1675):

Vanitas pictures:
1. Still Life, undated.
2. Niche in Trompe-l'œil, 1669.
3. Trompe-l'œil of a Trompe-l'œil, 1659/60-1675.

Oils on canvas.

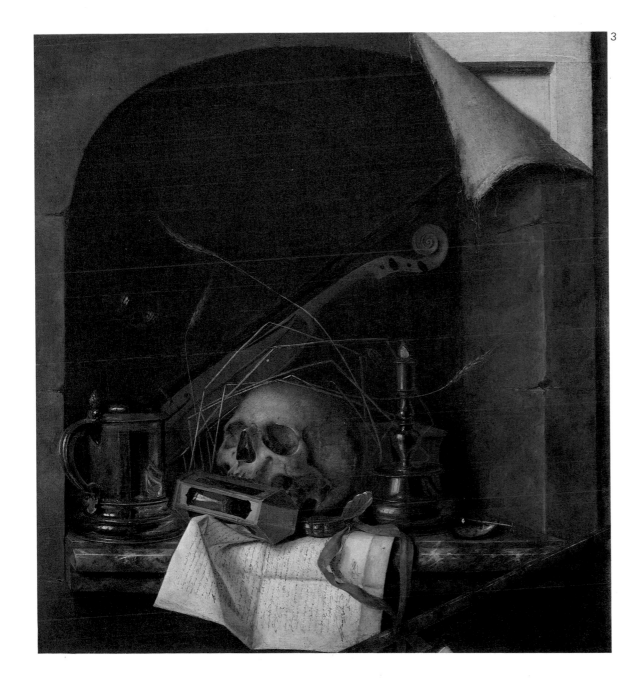

3

4 The discovery of the object

Employing the same means as wall painting but observing the rules we have just defined, trompe-l'œil easel painting will give the impression of depth either by hollowing out the wall to accommodate objects within it or by hanging them on the surface of the wall, projecting outwards. Representations of niches, shelves, or half-open cupboards offer us the quiet surprise of the reality which they lead us to discover.

the niche

The Flemish painters of the fifteenth century were the first to portray niches on the outer faces of their polyptych wings. These were an innovation in several respects. They created a trompe-l'œil, so presenting an *everyday* aspect to the owner of the altarpiece while concealing from him the vision of the icon on the inner side, which was exposed on feast days. The objects depicted were charged with a symbolism that was their justification for being associated with the object of worship. Usually we also find in them an interest in the object as such, stemming from a general trend towards a desacralization of the religious image in the countries of northern Europe.

The reverse of the *Braque Triptych* is possibly the earliest instance of this type of trompe-l'œil. Van der Weyden's altarpiece was commissioned by a young woman who had lost her husband one year after marrying him. The sombre, powerful image of the skull resting on a broken brick, standing out against the dark background of the niche, is accompanied by a lengthy inscription. The inscription clarifies the special meaning of this Vanitas, expressing as it does not only a reflection on death's destructiveness but also the bitterness of its injustice. [1] Paul Leprieur [2] calls it a "funereal *ex voto*, a token of love and devotion." It is by steeping ourselves in the message of the image—borne in upon us by its trompe-l'œil reality—that we grasp its underlying meaning. We know now that, though Catherine of Brabant soon remarried, she continued to venerate the altarpiece until her death. A special clause in her will left to her grandson what to the art historian remains a "triptych" but to her was a panel "with five images."

Rogier van der Weyden (1399-1464):
Braque Triptych, c. 1452:
Skull and Braque Armorial Bearings
on reverse of left wing.
Cross and Braque-Brabant Armorial
Bearings on reverse of right wing.
Oil on panels.

Attributed to Dirk Bouts (c. 1410/20-1475):
Niche with Books and Basin,
reverse of the "Virgin and Child,"
c. 1475. Oil on panel.

The attributes of the Virgin on their own [3] make up a trompe-l'œil still life on the reverse of a *Virgin and Child* panel attributed to Dirk Bouts. The gleaming basin half-protruding from the wall, the water we imagine the ewer to contain, the whiteness of the rumpled cloth and towel all symbolize the Virgin's purity. The casually opened book and the phylactery unrolling towards us bear witness to her learning and piety. [4] The towel-rail breaking into the spectator's space and the curtain just asking to be drawn serve to heighten the powerful reality of the whole.

Possibly less perfect in terms of integration in their surroundings than the niches in Gaddi's and Lorenzetti's frescoes, the ones that were painted on the reverse side of altarpieces for private devotions represent the kind of repertory and composition that were endlessly repeated over a whole series of trompe-l'œil easel paintings executed subsequently.

Barend van der Meer (?):
Cup and Bread in a Niche,
c. 1668. Oil on panel.

▷ Georg Flegel (1566-1638):
Still Life with Pipe.
Oil on panel.

Religious symbolism, directly bound up with the
attributes of the Saints and the mysteries of the
Church, continued to form, as it were, the spiritual
core (or pretext) of the earliest still lifes, though it later
became lost in the sheer number of objects depicted.
Yet the spiritual content is still very marked in the
simplicity of the trompe-l'œil niche painted by Barend
van der Meer at the end of the seventeenth century,
the bread and the glass of wine constituting an
obvious allusion to the Eucharist.
In the days when the Church's opprobrium extended
both to earthly goods and to their portrayal, St Anselm
(eleventh century) had preached that the danger
represented by "things" was in proportion to the
number of senses they affected. The Reformation,

while accepting the possession of things, [5] continued to emphasize their fragility, which accounts for the profusion of illustrations of the Vanitas theme produced in northern Europe in the seventeenth century. Originally mystical meditations on the passing of time and on death, they underwent a broadening of their symbolism over the years. [6] Drawing their iconography from the symbols of the period, they began to include allusions to the ephemerality of this world's riches and of the delights afforded by the senses.

Georg Flegel's *Still Life with Pipe*, for example, groups in a niche in the wall symbols of smell, of taste, of time being consumed like the wick of a lamp, but also a glass of wine; this may be a Eucharistic reference, but it is certainly also a mirror of the world of the spectator, who thus finds himself projected into the centre of this meditation.

Michel-Ange Houasse (1680-1730):
Two Trompe-l'œil Paintings
with Statuettes, companion pieces.
Oils on canvas.

The niches by Michel-Ange Houasse, painted at a time when moralizing lessons were beginning to become more sophisticated, are striking for the force of the contrast between the dark background with its barely perceptible structure and the whiteness of the statues. Bathed in opalescent light, the objects were meant to stand out with almost tactile realism from the walls in which these trompe-l'œil niches might have been integrated. [7] Were they painted for Philip V of Spain for the sole purpose of asserting the perfection of a royal collector's treasures? Is their message a purely visual one? Yet these portrayals of a studied

elegance, imbued as they are with a mysterious spirituality and with a severity appropriate to the Spanish Counter-Reformation, ask to be read on a different level. The riderless horse and the handsome young man turning away from his mirror recall the sin of pride and the vanity of possessions whose beauty will be obliterated by time. [8] The watch suggests this; the statuettes of the flute-playing youth, the wrestling adult, and the grimacing old man illustrate it. The trompe-l'œil quality of these works enhances their power of suggestion, the strangeness of visual and conceptual uncertainty adding to the interest of the thoughts they provoke.

Flemish School (16th century):
Still Life in a Cupboard, 1538.
Oil on panel.

△△ Master of the Aix Annunciation
(active c. 1445 in Provence):
Still Life with Books in a Niche,
upper part of "The Prophet Isaiah."
Oil on panel.

The niche, with its height and depth, calls for a perspective treatment, which tends to weaken the feeling of reality. It has often been replaced by the representation of a recess in the wall fitted with shelves laden with objects.

The idea had been clearly stated in the mid-fifteenth century in the still lifes that accompany the *Prophets* painted by the Master of the Aix Annunciation. [9] One of the precursors of this theme, he sets out on a shelf a pile of books, objects penetrating the spectator's space, and half-open manuscripts with ruffled pages, all contributing to the *realism* of a scholarly disorder. It is worth drawing attention to the fact that this disorderly arrangement of objects became a constant feature of trompe-l'œil painting. The implication of transience gives it a symbolic significance which relates it to the Vanitas theme. [10] It has also been judiciously pointed out that it suggests the incessant touch of human hands absent from the picture. [11] Nevertheless, it should not be forgotten that the choice of such a grouping of objects with neither symmetry nor single vanishing point is highly effective in creating a three-dimensional feeling. Thus the structure of the painting is not dictated by the subject alone, but is strongly dependent on the visual effect desired.

One finds the same accumulation of objects in the cupboard painted by an anonymous sixteenth-century Flemish artist. There is every indication that this panel decorated the door of an actual cupboard and that it presented a trompe-l'œil image of the everyday reality it concealed. And yet the candle is extinguished and there is a mouse nibbling at the loaf... Another moral lesson, perhaps?

The contemporary artist Henri Cadiou has painted some kitchen shelves that, with obvious nostalgia for the past, capture the same familiar yet remote, commonplace and yet magical atmosphere as the anonymous Flemish master's cupboard. This trompe-l'œil, however, offers us a harsher, more peremptory world, our world—and the artist's—as reflected in the shiny curves of the coffee pot.

Henri Cadiou (1906):
Kitchen Shelf, 1963.
Oil on panel.

Jean Valette-Penot (1710-after 1777):
Trompe-l'œil Cabinet with Statuette of Hercules.
Oil on canvas.

◁ Johann Georg Hainz
(second half of the 17th century):
Cabinet of Curiosities.
Oil on canvas.

The *Kunstkammerschrank* or "curio cabinet" pictures of the seventeenth and eighteenth centuries also belong to this group.

Johann Georg Hainz depicted a set of shelves made to measure to accommodate a selection of the treasures of the king of Denmark.[12] This display of wealth—from the glass engraved with the king's name to the jewellery and from the precious shell to the sculpted vase—epitomizes the *anti-Vanitas*. A miniature skull seeks vainly to remind us of the ephemeral nature of these possessions, since the trompe-l'œil technique employed makes them look utterly real. Apart from the volume suggested by the *rendering* of individual objects, the light picking out the ivory vase in the centre in contrast to the dark background gives a realer feeling of depth than any perspective construction would have done. This

painting, which was probably hung in the place set aside for the exhibition of the royal collections, was intended to dazzle and amaze the spectator by its double nature as false reality and deceptive image.

The rustic appearance—due to the undressed boards—of Jean Valette-Penot's *Cabinet* conceals a perfect eclecticism,[13] for the shelves carry objects from each of the three domains sought after by the accomplished collector. On them we find mechanical and art objects *(Artificialia)*, classical statuary *(Antiquitas)*, and above all shells, butterflies, snakes, and potions *(Naturalia)*. This trompe-l'œil, painted for a humanist who dabbled in science, needed to be hung in a very precise relationship to a light source because the strong lighting from the right in the picture, which virtually duplicates each object, dictates the position from which it is to be viewed.[14]

library of the Conservatorio di Musica G.B. Martini in Bologna. This skilful composition moves from the stiff verticals of the top shelf, with their suggestion of order, through the increasing disorder of the lower shelves to the muddle at the bottom implying the presence of man,[15] a presence that is further underlined by the inkwell, the pen, and the wipers for cleaning it. The painting bears warm witness to a bygone moment.

The books and objects in *The Bookcase* painted by Kenneth Davies are suggestive of a reality of which it forms part. The titles of the books, lit by harsh sunlight, are so many clues to a woman's life; we can guess at her preoccupations, we know of her sporting achievements, we even have her cigarette, left only a moment ago, its ash projecting over the edge and about to fall on our fingers. Trompe-l'œil here becomes the portrait of an individual through the medium of the objects around her.

Shelves loaded with treasures of various kinds (they might well be stuffed birds caught in their multi-coloured moment of death) make periodic reappearances each time trompe-l'œil comes back into fashion. Not greatly in favour with nineteenth-century American painters, the subject has been treated several times by the contemporary English painter Martin Battersby in what are now referred to as decorative panels.

Bookshelves are one variant of this type of picture. The contents, including the titles of the books, are often chosen to suit the place where the painting is hung, adding an *intellectual* argument to the *visual* one. The *Shelves with Music Books* by Giuseppe Maria Crespi, for example, was painted to hang in the

Kenneth Davies (1925):
The Bookcase, 1951.
Oil on canvas.

△ Giuseppe Maria Crespi (1665-1747):
Shelves with Music Books, 1710.
Oil on canvas.

◁ Alexandre-Isidore Leroy de Barde (1777-1828):
Collection of Foreign Birds, 1810.
Watercolour and gouache.

the half-open cupboard

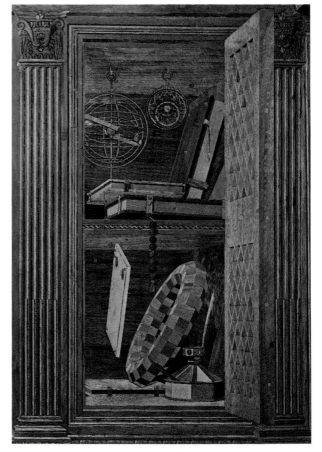

Showing one or more doors ajar lent greater credibility to the portrayal of wall cupboards while heightening the mysterious aspect of the work concerned. From the technical point of view such half-open doors, by invading the spectator's space, immediately give depth to a painting without creating problems of perspective. At the same time they throw into shadow the difficult background zone of the space depicted.

This solution was adopted to marvellous effect in the *studioli* of Renaissance palaces. Around the 1460s marquetry technique became particularly refined thanks to the boiled-wood process invented by the Landinara brothers. In the words of André Chastel,[16] "the crystalline space of the Quattrocento, centred and squared and all edges and *intersecazioni*, is in fact originally an *intarsia* space." The trick of inlaying pieces of wood of regular shape and delicately shaded colouring perfectly suited the game of perspective and the fashion for things geometrical. *Intarsie* were among the earliest self-contained portrayals of inanimate objects, and their influence was decisive —north of the Alps as well as to the south—as far as the developing iconography and composition of the still life were concerned.[17] Moreover we often find in them a deliberate intention to "deceive the eye."

Francesco di Giorgio Martini (1439-1502) and Baccio Pontelli (1450-1495): Studiolo of Federigo da Montefeltro, Duke of Urbino, △◁ in the Palazzo Ducale, Gubbio; △ in the Palazzo Ducale, Urbino. Panelling with intarsia.

Baccio Pontelli (1450-1495):
Studiolo of Federigo da Montefeltro,
Duke of Urbino, in the Palazzo
Ducale, Urbino.
Panelling with intarsia.

Though its success is questionable in the case of isolated objects, *intarsia* was capable of creating a very special kind of reality when used to cover completely the walls of that world apart, the *studiolo*. [18] Half-open cupboards create visual breaks in the panelling of these tiny rooms set aside for intellectual pursuits. Their doors, startlingly true to life, open onto a strange world in which death, faith, the *tempus fugit* theme, but also music and the sciences all blend in disturbing confusion. They provoke thought about the harmony of the humanist world but also about the temporality of its stirring intellectual preoccupations. [19] For the spectator, who finds himself completely cut off from the world by all these marquetry "messages," [20] what is created is a self-contained reality in which elements rendered in monochrome trompe-l'œil (that is to say, having little objective *credibility)* are spell-bindingly present.

Intarsie depicting the same objects and the same compositions as those used in the *studiolo* are still being made today. [21] Removed from their context and stripped of their conceptual content and their three-dimensional volume, they are meant to be—and succeed in being—the perfect ornamentation for furniture. But as mere decorative elements whose purpose is to camouflage, they are no more than quotations from trompe-l'œil.

In a different vein, two centuries after the Renaissance *intarsie*, Domenico Remps (?) opened wide the double doors of a cabinet to reveal the treasures of a famous collector.[22] The cut-out shape of this trompe-l'œil is a contributory factor in giving the spectator an irrepressible urge to step closer for a better look... or even to touch. Here the artist has used the *entire* vocabulary of the genre: superposition of surfaces, broken glass, the painting of a painting, the bas-relief medallion, the nail, crumpled paper... In its extreme virtuosity this is the pictorial equivalent of a "purple passage"—and we are a little annoyed at having been taken in by it.

Mirroring the specific reality of a certain way of life in nineteenth-century America, John Frederick Peto's open cupboard offers the "treasures" of a grocery store. The simplicity of the composition, the objects depicted, and above all the colouring conjure up a patriarchal yet primitive atmosphere with a strong whiff of childhood and innocence.

The representation of works of art

Grisaille has been employed since classical times to produce highly deceptive imitations of marble statuary. We have already analysed the fashion for and very successful use of this technique in wall painting and for decorative purposes.

As regards easel painting, one may mention the use that fifteenth-century Flemish painters made of grisaille to decorate the backs of their polyptych wings. Initially, to give the altarpiece the content and appearance of the complete object of worship, the outer face depicted (in the manner of the church porch) niches containing statues painted in grisaille. [1] This was also a way of liberating painters in their attempts to represent space, which, in the main panels, were still tied down to the rigid constraints of the icon and its celestial world.

painting and sculpture

◁ Jan van Eyck (c. 1385/90-1441):
The Annunciation, diptych.
The Angel of the Annunciation, left wing.
The Virgin Mary, right wing.
Oil on panels.

Master of the Aix Annunciation
(active c. 1445 in Provence):
The Prophet Isaiah.
Oil on panel.

Marvellously moulded and firmly planted on their bases, Jan van Eyck's Angel and Virgin stand out against the precious, polished backgrounds in which they are reflected. Though the statues are set in niches, the Angel's wing sticks out and casts a shadow on the frame. The light falling from the right unifies and sanctifies the group. It was perhaps this subtle perfection about Van Eyck's *Annunciation* that made it the principal object of veneration in a diptych for private devotion. For the reverses of these panels, which are decorated with the same imitation of porphyry as the frames, do not open on any painting.

Statues painted in grisaille subsequently fell into the trap set by the liberties taken by their creators. They began to "come alive" [2] and even to take on colour, as in the case of the *Prophets* on the wings of the *Aix Annunciation* altarpiece. In acquiring the breath of life, these portrayals of statues seem to lose their trompe-l'œil effect.

We ought, however, to ask ourselves whether this view is not a product of our projecting the grey world of our present-day cities onto these works from the past. It is in fact hard for us to imagine how much the Late Middle Ages blazed with a colourfulness quite unknown today. [3] But if fifteenth-century statues were coloured, what was the reality that these trompe-l'œil grisailles reflected? Was it the drabness of the ordinary, non-feast days when altarpieces were closed? Research has yet to find the answer. [4]

Giovanni Francesco Penni
(c. 1488-1528):
Abundance.
Grisaille on panel.

There is an interesting grisaille by Giovanni Francesco Penni that is documented as having served as a cover for Raphael's *Small Holy Family*.[5] The beautifully executed figure of *Abundance* stands out like a statuette from its background of mock inlaid marble, showing how in Italy such covering panels continued to be done in trompe-l'œil.

Painted panels imitating bas-reliefs were very much in fashion as early as the end of the seventeenth century. Beginning with Jacob De Wit—the Dutch master who made *witjes* ("white," in Dutch) fashionable in France—the school continued through Geeraerts, Sauvage, Doncre, and Boilly,[6] all of whom decorated church and palace walls with large panels. The impact of these works is absolutely amazing, the artists having succeeded with equal virtuosity in depicting both high-relief and sculpture in the round, degrees of depth as well as the quality of movement.

Both patrons and artists in eighteenth-century France were certainly very much interested in the painted imitation of classical or neo-classical bas-reliefs. [7] Today we tend to look down on this kind of trompe-l'œil as mere decoration, yet such works were the expression of an art that was much appreciated and practised very widely. They were placed above doors and often in the centre of the room above the fireplace. Artists of the calibre of Sauvage, Oudry, and Chardin painted them with obvious enthusiasm, and there is a wealth of contemporary critical evidence to show how popular they were at court and among visitors to the Salons. [8] In creating such works, an artist as original as Chardin must undoubtedly have been paying homage to sculpture—or to the contemporary sculptor—and taking up Leonardo's challenge to do as well, if not better, with means that were *a priori* unsuitable.

Some of these works were reproduced so *faithfully* that the artists did not hesitate to include cracks or, like the Genevan François Ferrière, dusty frames eaten away by cockroaches.

Nicolas-Guy Brenet (1728-1792):
Allegory of Roman Justice, 1760.
Grisaille. Oil on canvas.

François Ferrière (1752-1839):
Poetry: Cupids.
Oil on canvas.

Ferrarese School (15th century):
Madonna and Child with Two Angels, c. 1480.
Oil on panel.

In representing a painting in the trompe-l'œil manner, the artist is freed of all constraints of veracity as far as the *content* of the picture is concerned. It is only the *container*, the vehicle, that need "deceive the eye."

To turn a painting into a *trompe-l'œil of a painting* the artist has to introduce a *repoussoir*, a strong foreground element that will visually and intellectually relegate the content to the acceptedly fictitious world of the image. The painting has to become an object, and it is this object that receives the trompe-l'œil treatment. The *repoussoir* may be a curled-up corner of the canvas,[9] a frayed edge, a broken pane of glass, an imaginary frame, or of course a more complicated setting.

The painting by the Ferrarese School shows that the suggestive potential of the *painting of a painting* was appreciated as early as 1480. It represents a conventional holy picture, painted on the back of a canvas, which was once covered with a cloth attached by tapes nailed to the frame. The cloth has been ripped away, so that only the torn edges can be seen, revealing the vision of the *Virgin and Child*. Artists have often interpreted the concept of revelation almost literally as a *lifting of the veil*. In this extraordinary trompe-l'œil the spectator finds himself directly implicated in an act of violence that enables him to apprehend the Divinity.

Through its power of evocation this painting raises the reality/fiction ambivalence to heights of great spiritual richness. A surprising work in the artistic context of Quattrocento Italy, it anticipates by two centuries the use of the backs of pictures, torn material, and nailed-up tapes as a kind of alphabet of trompe-l'œil painting. [10]

The Dutch had a marvellous *repoussoir* ready to hand for turning a painting into a trompe-l'œil. This was the curtain that they commonly used to protect their paintings from light and dust. Gerard Dou made extensive use of it, and his trompe-l'œil *Self-Portrait* emerging from behind a false curtain offers the most perfect illustration. [11] Whether the painting is of a landscape or a bunch of flowers, the curtain in the foreground occupies part of the spectator's space. This gives it the significance of a reality and pushes the image itself back into the realm of illusion. Rembrandt, for example, did not hesitate to use a curtain to cover a corner of one of his biblical scenes. [12]

Gerrit Houckgeest's painting, in using the curtain as if to separate two spaces, raises questions that are left unanswered. Is what we are looking at a *painting* with its protective curtain, or is this the view from a window that—oddly—gives into a church? In other words, is it a trompe-l'œil depiction of a painting or an illusionist depiction of a reality? The *painting of a painting* theme gives a glimpse here of its enormous resources.

Gerrit Houckgeest (c. 1580/90-1661):
Interior of the Oude Kerk in Delft,
c. 1650. Oil on panel.

Adriaen van der Spelt (c. 1630-1673):
Flower Piece with Curtain, 1658.
Oil on panel.

59

Angolo del Moro (active late 16th century):
Vision of the Holy Family near Verona,
1581. Oil on canvas.

In his *Vision of the Holy Family near Verona*, Angolo del Moro [13] shows a canvas coming away from its support. The top is rolled back on itself in a way that prevents us from seeing the whole of the painting depicting the *Vision* against a cloudy sky overlooking a distant view of Verona. In contrast, the folded *cartellino* vouches as usual for the painting's belonging to the world of pictorial representation. Yet behind the rolled-back edge we see the rest of the picture, perceiving it as a *reality* of which the painting is a mere replica. It is in *undeceiving* the spectator that this painting becomes a trompe-l'œil.

Almost four centuries later Magritte raised the problem in a similar way by interposing a third plane of reality. If the spectator *enters* Magritte's *The*

Human Condition I, he finds himself faced with a canvas that he cannot distinguish from the landscape before which it stands. He is looking at a perfect trompe-l'œil. For the perceptive spectator who looks at it from a certain distance, the game is given away by the white band where the canvas is tacked to the side of the stretcher and by the top of the easel. This twofold portrayal of an outer world and an inner world, a vision and a reality (which is itself artificial), gives the subject that infinite richness of interpretation that is one of the qualities of Surrealism. We touch here on one of the subtlest contemporary aspects of trompe-l'œil, which in the words of Fabrizio Clerici aims ''to astonish, to dazzle and hallucinate'' at one and the same time. [14]

René Magritte (1898-1967):
The Human Condition I, 1934.
Oil on canvas.

trompe-l'œil, drawings, prints

The idea of representing drawings and prints in paint undoubtedly offered artists a tempting challenge, that of using brush and colour to convey the graphic quality of black and white. Here was confirmation of the superiority of painting over drawing; here too was freedom to choose one's *subject* as in any portrayal of a work of art while simulating depth with the aid of the suggestiveness of paper, which could be stacked, folded, torn—whatever the artist wished. This type of picture made it possible to build up a whole system of quotations in which trompe-l'œil paintings were made of engravings by the artist—occasionally reproducing his own works—or done by professional engravers from well-known paintings. It became a kind of punning with images. Tributes to the diversity of the artist's own talent or to that of others, these trompe-l'œil works tell us as much about their creator's virtuosity as about the taste of a period.

Depicting drawings and engravings in a jumble of papers of different textures enabled Wallerant Vaillant to bring off the feat of his *"Four Sides."* Cards and prints overlap one another in bewildering confusion, making it a matter of indifference which way up the painting is hung. Closer examination reveals the artificial nature of the composition. The ostensibly random assemblage is in fact an intricate arrangement, so intricate that it would probably be impossible to achieve in reality.

Wallerant Vaillant (1623-1677):
"Four Sides."
Oil on canvas.

▷ Gabriel Gresly (1712-1756):
Trompe-l'œil with "Almanach du solitaire,"
c. 1750. Oil on canvas.

Gresly's trompe-l'œil takes up again a familiar composition of the painter's.[15] A print is fixed with nails and sealing wax to a knotted, grainy plank of wood. Badly torn and no longer of any artistic interest, it is there only to support an envelope and a pen. Yet *The Surgeon* must have enjoyed a certain fame for we find the print depicted in a number of trompe-l'œil paintings.[16] An equally ancient and dog-eared book is hanging from a nail below it. Is there some connection between the *Almanach du solitaire*, the print, and the letter addressed to a priest? The web of meaning underlying this trompe-l'œil has itself been destroyed by time, and we are left simply with this harmony of muted tones blending wood-grain and battered papers into a delightful whole.

Louis Boilly, who was fascinated by problems of optics and made innovative contributions to trompe-l'œil techniques, left an interesting *Self-Portrait with Broken Glass* in grey monochrome. A perfect imitation of a print, it might well have deceived the eye *totally*. The subterfuge of the *perfect* trompe-l'œil could in theory pass unnoticed.[17] This is where the broken glass comes in. By attracting the spectator's attention, it makes him step closer and read the signature that holds the key to the mystery: the work is signed *Boilly pinxit*, not *Boilly incidit*.

Louis Léopold Boilly (1761-1845):
Self-Portrait with Broken Glass, c. 1805-1810.
Grisaille. Oil on paper mounted on canvas.

the painting and its frame

The frame of a painting may be regarded as the ornament around it as well as the place or the setting in which it is exhibited. In both cases trompe-l'œil poses some ambiguous problems.

Occasionally a trompe-l'œil painting will incorporate its own mock frame. If it depicts a frayed canvas or one that has come away from its stretcher, it ought not to be framed; museums today should respect this logical consequence of its iconography. Similarly a work of art hung on a wooden panel has no need of a frame.

Often the work of art is surrounded by other objects in a composition that is rarely left to chance. This may give us a glimpse of the character of the person who commissioned the picture and enable us to guess at the sort of surroundings in which it would have been presented. Gresly's painting, which we looked at just now, must have fitted very readily into the hermit priest's presbytery. Doncre's cherubs symbolizing the Art of Drawing (in the purest Boucher manner) were adapted by the artist to suit the life-style and personality of the Dunkerque goldsmith Guillaume Bert. [18] The patron's presence is evoked for our benefit by his playing cards, his pince-nez, and the letter addressed to him.

Dominique Doncre (1743-1820):
Trompe-l'œil with Putti.
Oil on canvas.

Cornelis Norbertus Gijsbrechts
(c. 1610-after 1675):
Studio Wall with Vanitas, 1668.
Oil on canvas.

▷ Benedetto Sartori
(active mid-18th century):
Studio Wall and Shelf with
the Painter's Attributes.
Oil on canvas.

But there is one kind of *setting* that remains difficult to rationalize. This concerns a whole series of trompe-l'œil paintings evoking the artist's studio.

In the painting by Cornelis Gijsbrechts we find the same Vanitas that he depicted as a still life, as a trompe-l'œil niche, and as a trompe-l'œil of the trompe-l'œil niche. This time it is accompanied by the tools of the artist's trade and by three miniatures, one of which is presumably his self-portrait. The mahlstick, which seems to be cut off by the edge of the picture, does not in fact constitute an infringement of the rules. It appears that the work was mutilated to make it fit into a conventional frame.[19] Originally this must have been a *cut-out*, with the silhouette of the

mahlstick projecting beyond the edge of the panel. The corner of Benedetto Sartori's studio[20] shows not only the painter's tools but also two successive stages of artistic creation. This may be a reminder of the passing of time, like the extinguished lamp; it is also an affirmation of the artist's versatility as painter and engraver.

Do these pictures, so deeply imbued with the artist's personality—bringing a picturesque corner of the studio into the purchaser's house—manage to transcend their role as mirrors of reality? Were they placed in that alien environment precisely in order to provoke surprise at their incongruity and consequently admiration at their success? We do not know.

A photograph is certainly regarded as giving, in two dimensions, the most exact replica of reality. Yet is it capable of taking the place of reality, if only for an instant?

When Brunelleschi invented the screen with a central aperture that enabled him to construct exact perspective for the first time, he was in fact using a *camera obscura* with monocular vision—the basic principle behind the photographic camera. [21] Obviously, then, a photograph will be subject to the same limitations as a picture constructed in perspective, notably that of the single viewpoint, which is alien to the physiology of human vision.

Paradoxically, for a photograph to be capable of taking the place of reality, that is to say of "deceiving the eye," it must conform to the rules of trompe-l'œil. It is required, in other words, to be a *photograph of a trompe-l'œil.* This is what Braun's photograph shows us, presenting as it does objects standing out against a plank of wood, recreating the typical "hunting trophy" of traditional trompe-l'œil painting. The result is not entirely successful, however, because photography, unlike oil painting, is incapable of rendering the texture of objects in ways that transcend its own substance. It is imprisoned behind the barrier that the painter breaks through when—in Martin Battersby's words [22]—he goes on to intensify shadows and make highlights more brilliant.

painting
and
photography

Audrey Flack (1931):
Family Portrait, 1969-1970.
Oil on canvas.

◁ Adolphe Braun (1811-1877):
Still Life with Hare and Ducks, 1859.
Photograph, collodion negative.

On the other hand, if Braun's photograph recreated one of the classic compositions of seventeenth and eighteenth-century trompe-l'œil painting, it also inspired in its turn the pictures that the American painter William Michael Harnett entitled *After the Hunt*.[23] This interaction is possibly symptomatic of the change in *style* and *rendering* that came over trompe-l'œil painting with the advent of photography, an influence whose results can perhaps be regarded as dubious.

Super-realist art has brought out a new relationship between photography and trompe-l'œil. The process that consists in projecting a photograph onto a canvas and painting the resultant image enables us to call such a picture as Audrey Flack's a *trompe-l'œil of a photograph*.

When it becomes the trompe-l'œil of a work of art, super-realism can occasionally delude.

the negation
of the painting

Cornelis Norbertus Gijsbrechts
(c. 1610-after 1675):
Turned-over Canvas, c. 1670.
Oil on canvas.

William M. Davis (1829-1920):
A Canvas Back, c. 1870.
Oil on canvas.

▷ Pierre Ducordeau (1928):
"Picture on Loan," 1974.
Oil on canvas.

The artist of the Ferrarese School used the back of a painting to *reveal* a celestial vision. Gijsbrechts, in his extraordinary *Turned-over Canvas*, depicts the blank back of a painting, which represents a total negation of the work of art. Designed to be exhibited on the floor, propped against a wall,[24] this painting constitutes an irresistible provocation to the spectator to turn it round in order to look at *the painted side*, which is non-existent. The height of cerebral paradox, it implies its own negation and is like a slap in the face to the art lover. Perhaps it is also prophetically symbolic of the neglect that Gijsbrechts' whole œuvre was to suffer for centuries, turned to the wall in the cellars of the world's museums. Neither William M. Davis nor John Frederick Peto is likely to have seen

Gijsbrechts' work. Yet on the other side of the Atlantic they took up the theme of the picture turned to the wall. By adding envelopes bearing the artist's name, making puns,[25] or pinning up a portrait of Lincoln,[26] the American artists gained greater relief and an extra anecdotal element, but they broke the powerful spell of the Gijsbrechts painting.

An empty frame casts a shadow on the white wall behind it: Pierre Ducordeau's *Self-Portrait* has been removed for inclusion in a London exhibition of "French Masterpieces." It needs the humorous note of the "picture on loan" chit tucked between mount and frame to draw the spectator back from the fascinating, dizzying white oval void left by the missing picture.

The triumph
of
objects

Niches and cupboards hold objects within their shadowy depths *beyond* the wall surface. The projecting elements in trompe-l'œil paintings, on the other hand, and mock bas-reliefs whose convexities catch the light demonstrate the powerful physical presence of objects represented as being *this side of* the wall. The three-dimensional effect of objects that *invade* the spectator's space made itself felt as early as the fifteenth century in the device known as the *cartellino*, but it became positively obtrusive in the depiction of papers, books, and instruments of all kinds that embellished the cells of holy men dedicated to the intellectual life. We find it in Flemish paintings but also in Venice, in the work of Bellini and above all in Carpaccio. [1] Thus it is not surprising that it should have been Carpaccio, a painter who was obsessed by the presence of objects, who painted one of the very earliest self-contained trompe-l'œil pictures that have come to light. This is a wooden panel which must surely have served as a cupboard door, but the bottom

the letter rack
and
the quodlibet

Vitture Carpaccio (c. 1460/65-c. 1526):

▷ Hunting on the Lagoon, recto.

◁ Cornice with Letter Rack, verso.

Oil on panel.

of it is now cut off and missing. [2] A hunting scene is depicted on the recto, and on the verso we find a cornice with a length of tape holding letters and documents nailed across it. The work is damaged, but we can make out a name, probably that of the person who commissioned it. The painting is a true trompe-l'œil, constructed in accordance with the rules and depicting the objects that might actually have met the eye of anyone opening the door of the cupboard. Carpaccio anticipated by more than a century the kind of composition that later became almost synonymous with trompe-l'œil painting.

It was in fact towards the middle of the seventeenth century that representations of crumpled or folded papers fixed to a flat surface amongst other odds and ends became a favourite subject for trompe-l'œil. These papers, whether printed or handwritten, are usually vehicles of legible messages that lend them a certain physical credibility and prompt the spectator to try to decipher them. The presence of objects in such paintings is invariably charged with some meaning that may be symbolic and is often personal. In nearly every case the support is a panel. This material a painting could imitate superbly [3] and it combined well with existing panelling. Crackled and aged as much as the artist cared to make it, it also fitted into the Vanitas symbolism with which seventeenth and eighteenth-century trompe-l'œil was associated.

Even if we can no longer regard it as the earliest known letter-rack trompe-l'œil, Wallerant Vaillant's is nevertheless one of the finest. Here the tape is nailed criss-cross to a wooden panel and the letters are casually tucked behind it. The quill and stylet evoke the writer's hand, and a date is scrawled on the panel in chalk. The legible addresses and messages have lost their significance for us, though we do notice one letter addressed to a prince, who may have commissioned the painting. The composition is clearly defined by the geometrical figure formed by the tapes, which also establishes the shallow depth. The tapes seem to hold back the objects, which despite their

△ Wallerant Vaillant (1623-1677):
Letter Rack, 1658.
Oil on canvas.

▷ John Frederick Peto (1854-1907):
Card Rack with Jack of Hearts.
Oil on canvas.

apparent disorder are carefully balanced; some folded corners and the quill protrude towards the spectator to celebrate this modest victory in the conquest of space.

John Frederick Peto's card rack, which echoes the geometry of Vaillant's picture, gives the impression of being its ghost. Here everything is torn, neglected, abandoned. The photograph of Lincoln only indicates a date and, despite the aggressively coloured paper, the dark support has the significance of mourning. This is not a victory of the objects but the twofold defeat of the artist who has failed in life and the man of whom time has removed all trace. [4]

Another type of composition using tapes to hold a variety of objects including letters and printed matter against a wooden panel is the *quodlibet* or *vide-poches* ("pocket-emptyings"). Again, despite the apparent disorder, nothing is left to chance. The objects are shown life-size and are never very large, so that the rules of trompe-l'œil are observed and success assured. They are obvious reflections of everyday life, usually linked with the Vanitas symbolism and its corollary, the four senses. One of the most complicated examples of this kind of iconography is the *Quodlibet* (one of a great many) by Gijsbrechts. [5] Here is the whole arsenal of the genre. The scissors and knife allude to life's flimsy thread and the watch and almanac to time slipping away; the brush and comb symbolize the purification of the soul. The purse, jewels, and musical instruments are reminders of the futility of earthly possessions and the delights afforded by the senses. [6] Much to our relief, a curtain modestly conceals what threatens to become a pitiless recital of every human frailty.

Ultimately the question arises whether this vocabulary had not become so overloaded as to have lost all moral force, even for contemporaries. The charm of these pictures possibly lay in their familiarity, in the element of *déjà-vu* that brought the fragments of reality so close to the spectator's own experience.

Despite being produced in such numbers, quodlibets rarely became repetitive. Balance and credibility sometimes suffered because of the sheer quantity of objects depicted, but as documentary records of their time they remain fascinating reading. Artists on both sides of the Atlantic have been painting quodlibets from the seventeenth century to the present day.

A contemporary exponent is Claude Yvel, who describes lucidly and critically the world he lives in. He expresses himself not only through his selection of the reality that his pictures reflect but also through the forceful and incisive quality of his technique.

Against a background of painted wood that no longer suggests the Vanitas theme but evokes a particular social setting, we have the objects that fill the life of *The Schoolboy*. Those associated with work are ranged in a perfect order that we sense has been forced on the child but also serves to give the picture balance. It is through his out-of-school interests, through the objects that form the diagonal in the composition, that the schoolboy—and with him the spectator's eye—escapes coercion. The photograph of the child, the aeroplane drawing, the Batman figure, the pistol... the movement is towards the violence of the adult member of a society that Yvel's trompe-l'œil paintings condemn.

◁ Cornelis Norbertus Gijsbrechts
(c. 1610-after 1675):
Quodlibet, 1672.
Oil on canvas.

Claude Yvel (1930):
The Schoolboy, 1977.
Oil on canvas.

Through the objects represented, the quodlibet may sometimes call to mind not only a socio-cultural ambience but a personality, perhaps the artist's. Samuel van Hoogstraten's richly pictorial work possesses a luminosity and relief not often achieved in the still lifes of the period. His jumble of objects stands out sharply against a dark, abstract background that derives its credibility from the astonishingly deceptive frame. Here the plastic reality of objects reigns supreme.

This trompe-l'œil is also rich in content, revealing its secrets one by one to the spectator who allows himself to come under its spell. A first glance gives a warm feeling of being in touch with the reflection of a homely, cultured existence from a bygone age. A subsequent, moral reading finds that each object has its place in the symbolic programme of a Vanitas. Nevertheless, behind this iconography the artist is hinting at a reality both secret and profound, for his

trompe-l'œil is in fact the most revealing of self-portraits. The composition includes a reference to an important episode in Hoogstraten's life, when during a presentation of his paintings at the Viennese court the deceived and delighted emperor rewarded him with the decoration that figures prominently in the foreground. [7] The clearly legible alexandrines tell the story of the Greek painter Zeuxis, to whom the poet compares the artist. [8] If the pince-nez is the painter's, it betrays an infirmity that he never allowed to appear in his self-portraits. This physical defect is quickly blotted out by the presence of two literary works from Hoogstraten's pen. [9] He was the complete humanist: painter, writer, and art theorist. His writings show his condescending attitude to "papers and combs" depicted against a background of "panels or walls," which he dismissed as easy exercises for beginners. Yet in the same work he admitted that "honours" could be won by deceiving princes. In line with the academic thinking of the period, Hoogstraten placed historical scenes at the top of the hierarchy of values; trompe-l'œil and still life were at the bottom of the scale.[10]

Scorning, as a theorist, the "facility" of trompe-l'œil but as an artist experiencing obvious pleasure and pride in practising it, Hoogstraten gives us a glimpse of the real nature of a personality as ambivalent as the images he depicted and that made him famous.

Restrained, well-constructed, unostentatious, yet highly skilful, Dominique Doncre's *Letter Rack* is the very image of his character and œuvre. *Ego sum pictor*, he wrote beneath his grave and proud self-portrait. It was in a spirit of discreet self-congratulation and with no ulterior motive that he thus portrayed himself amid the tools of his trade, in a slightly worm-eaten frame that so perfectly matches his reality as a provincial "little master."[11]

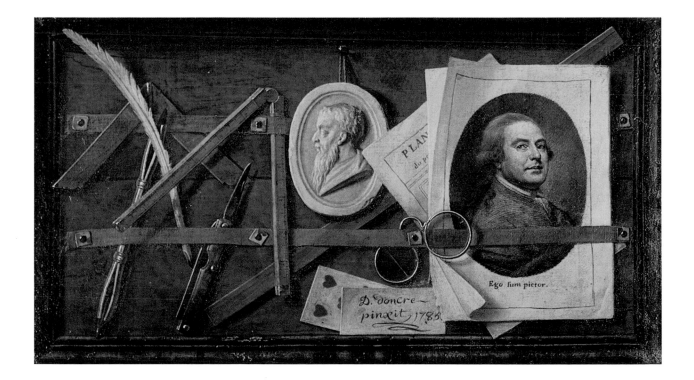

△ Dominique Doncre (1743-1820):
Letter Rack, 1785.
Oil on canvas.

◁ Samuel van Hoogstraten (1627-1678):
Quodlibet.
Oil on canvas.

trompe-l'œil
and
the pamphlet

The piece of paper bearing a written or graphic message in black and white is also suggestive of printing and the multiplication of its contents. The objects depicted sometimes become subordinate to the pamphlet aspect and reveal a particular stance in a situation of political conflict.

Edward Collier's *Letter Rack* uses a composition that he repeated many, many times. Only when we read the printed documents do we appreciate the difference in meaning. The knife, scissors, and almanac allude to the passing of time and the vulnerability of existence. The presence of the small medallion with its effigy of Charles I, beheaded fifty years earlier, was associated at the time with Vanitas symbolism [12] and served as a reminder of the ephemeral power of kings. Linking him with Queen Anne's speech to Parliament

Edward Collier (1640-after 1706):
Letter Rack, 1703.
Oil on canvas.

was tantamount to taking a stand in the religious dispute. The sympathies of the painter from Leyden, and those of his client, for the Protestant dynasty emerge as clearly as do the brightly lit objects against their dark background. The simplicity and sobriety of this trompe-l'œil fit the image of the Puritanism it conjures up.

The wooden panel as the painter's mouthpiece may bear only a single message. The *Ordonnance du Roi* ("Royal Decree") of Charles Lacroix is ripped right through, and what is left of it is pinned up with the aid of scraps of a playing card: the king of hearts. Painted in 1773, this trompe-l'œil is constructed with meticulous care, the print being legible both on the recto and—backwards—through the paper, telling anyone who wished to know where its creator's political allegiance lay. For whom can it have been intended, this proclamation of so personal and, for the period, so revolutionary a creed? [13]

In Laurent Dabos' painting the broken glass, pointing an accusing finger at Napoleon, is barely able to retain the weight of the papers sliding down behind it. Everything about this portrayal of the "Definitive Peace Treaty between France and Spain" is provisional. For at the time when the picture was painted the treaty was already meaningless and the Spanish insurrection had marked the beginning of the end of "la gloire napoléonienne." In the jargon of linguistics, the signifier is here in complete harmony with the signified. A true political pamphlet, Laurent Dabos' trompe-l'œil simultaneously reflects the reality of objects around him, the ideas of his time, and his own personal position vis-à-vis events.

Laurent Dabos (1761-1835):
"Traité de paix définitif entre la France et l'Espagne," after 1801.
Oil on canvas.

Charles Lacroix:
"Ordonnance du Roi," 1773.
Oil on canvas.

D. D. F. VANDESTEENE. 1818

hunting trophies

Hunting trophies, showing the remains of once-living creatures frozen in the stillness of death, were also depicted in trompe-l'œil. The famous *Partridge* painted by Jacopo de Barbari in 1504 is often cited as one of the first still lifes;[14] it is also one of the earliest examples of trompe-l'œil. It was followed by a striking number of trompe-l'œil paintings of game. Initially associated with Vanitas symbolism, they seem to have adorned bourgeois interiors as much as the palaces of royalty, the class that has always been keen on hunting.

The sight of dead birds nailed by their feet and hanging head downwards, sometimes embellished by gaudy plumage or a coloured ribbon, invariably has something dramatic about it. The claws and splayed wings of Francis van Myerop's bird almost constitute an assault on the spectator, and the alarming realism of this trompe-l'œil makes one shrink back involuntarily.

Commissioning paintings of deer-hunting trophies seems to have been a royal idea. When on 3 July 1741 the royal hunt took a hart of ten with an oddly shaped head, Louis XV summoned his animal painter to immortalize it. Oudry, then at the height of his fame, had the idea of presenting the trophy in trompe-l'œil against a background of wooden boards with a *cartellino* reporting the event. Oudry's talent emerges even through this unprepossessing subject, and one can well appreciate that the king should have preferred such pictures to the vulgar realism of the mounted antlers decorating the hunting rooms of ordinary mortals. This trompe-l'œil was the start of a collection of paintings by Oudry, Bachelier, and Perdrix extending over two reigns from 1741 to 1778. It was to adorn the semicircular staircase serving Louis XV's private apartments and may have been a late French adaptation of the *Schatzkammer* of Nordic courts.[15]

Jean-Baptiste Oudry (1686-1755):
Antlers of a Stag Taken by the
King on 3 July 1741.
Oil on canvas.

◁ Francis van Myerop (1640-1690):
Still Life with Bird, c. 1670.
Oil on canvas.

Cornelis Norbertus Gijsbrechts
(c. 1610-after 1675):
Trophy of Musical Instruments, 1672.
Oil on canvas.

◁ William Michael Harnett (1848-1892):
After the Hunt, 1885.
Oil on canvas.

Dead animals nailed to a wooden panel were among the subjects depicted by the pioneers of American trompe-l'œil in the years following 1800 as well as by its second school of painters fifty years later.[16]

In his famous *After the Hunt* paintings William Michael Harnett depicted bag, weapons, and instruments all suspended against a wooden background together with a horseshoe, a flask, and the hunter's hat. Thus, with these extra objects, the artist brought in a human presence as well as a specifically local way of life. This type of trompe-l'œil is a true piece of Americana.

Hunting and death are far away... What is left is a similar sort of composition in which objects suspended from a single point are at once concentrated and dispersed in a dynamic falling movement. Hanging from a nail against a piece of wood, every vein, knot, and split of which is rendered with startling fidelity.

Gijsbrechts' collection of musical instruments is also—curiously—called a *Trophy*. The portrayal of musical instruments had its origin in the *intarsie* of the Renaissance, but with Gijsbrechts these objects emerged from their hiding place in the wall to lay their elegant shapes one on top of another, the sinuous curves of violin, guitar, and harp alternating with the straight lines of flute and bow. A.P. de Mirimonde, who has made a special study of them, has deciphered their symbolism, identified them, and drawn attention to their importance as musicological documents. [17]

In contrast to these trophies, the fowler's equipment painted with stern symmetry by Johannes Leemans offers us a world in repose. The objects are waiting; the action has yet to take place. The empty cage and the game pouch catch all the light and stand out solidly in three dimensions. The virtually monochrome composition of objects fixed to the wall along immutable, repetitive verticals and horizontals is symptomatic of its being mass-produced. It represents the oddly abstract reality of an organization rigidly nailed down and a harmony of shapes and volumes that finds a resonant echo in the musical instruments that are invariably included. Unlike the sumptuous hunting trophies that Gijsbrechts painted for his royal patron, the weapons and instruments depicted here are those of the middle classes for whom such trompe-l'œil paintings were intended.

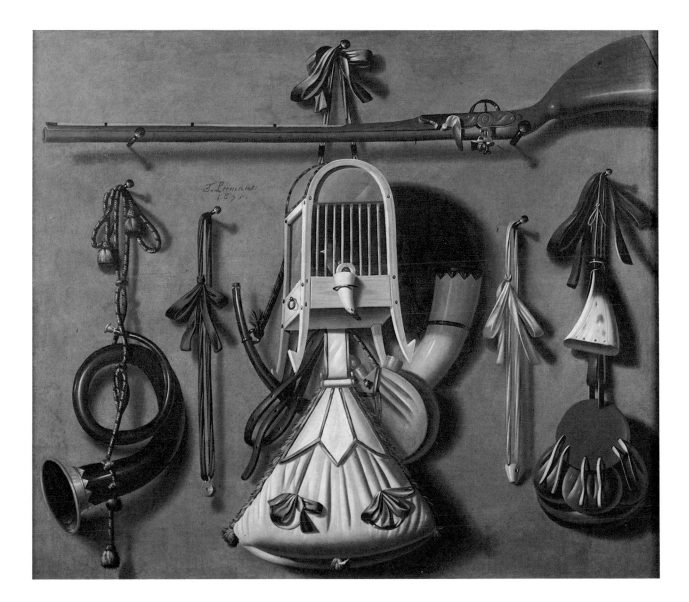

Johannes Leemans (c. 1633-c. 1688):
Attributes of the Fowler, 1675.
Oil on canvas.

7

Deceptive objects

Leaving the wall to which it is supposed to adapt itself, the trompe-l'œil can be, or belong to, a piece of *furniture*, as defined in the eighteenth century: a movable object of rigid form which goes to fit up the house.

The trompe-l'œil can also assume the aspect of an object, without actually being one. When, in this form, it takes its place in space, its position and definition become ambiguous. This chapter—rashly perhaps—will touch on the hazy borderline that separates art from ornament, object from sculpture, and reality from fiction.

Cornelis Norbertus Gijsbrechts
(c. 1610-after 1675):
Cupboard Door in Trompe-l'œil,
1670.
Interior and exterior.
Oil on canvas.

▷ Attributed to Jan van der Vaart
(1647-1721):
Painted Violin.
Oil on canvas mounted on panel.

trompe-l'œil and furniture

The extraordinary success with which painters imitated wood led to the integration of trompe-l'œil directly into furniture. It often served as a cupboard or closet door. [1] It is quite possible that many trompe-l'œil panel paintings, now regarded as independent pictures, were originally used in this way, as door panels.

Carrying the deception, as always, as far as possible, Gijsbrechts painted, by way of a door for a real cupboard, a simulated pane of glass with a letter rack strung across it. Here he combined an assortment of letters, cards, and a quill pen, placed between the strap and the glass pane, some of the objects projecting out from the plane of the door. Opening this cupboard door, one is confronted on its back with the reverse side of reality: now the glass window has moved into the foreground, and behind this transparent surface one sees in back view the very same objects, the shapes and positions coinciding exactly. This double-sided trompe-l'œil attempts not only to solve the problem of the third dimension but also to disclose the hidden underside of things, which the eye does not see but which the mind is well aware of. Taking us by surprise and prompting us to act, this painting of three centuries ago has lost none of its freshness.

Less interesting in its conception but very skilfully executed, the *Painted Violin* attributed to Jan van der Vaart was painted on a door panel for Devonshire House in London and removed a century later to Chatsworth. It has now been inserted in a locked door which closes off the music room, and there it is seen through the narrow opening of a real door. The result of this *perfect* display of a *perfect* trompe-l'œil is that unknowing visitors take it for an actual violin hanging on the door and pass by unsuspectingly, with no more than a glance at it. An *actual* trompe-l'œil *in situ* passing unnoticed: has it achieved its purpose?

When wholly subordinated to furniture and integrated into it, the trompe-l'œil may become a purely decorative element. In this way monochrome painting has been used to imitate pieces of sculptured bronze[2] and paintings in grisaille have taken the place of marble and ivory inlays. An example of outstanding quality is the Louis XVI writing table stamped "J. Dubois," which probably belonged to Marie-Antoinette.[3]

In the eighteenth century, probably in Florence, some tables were covered with *commessi* in hard stone, after designs by Charles-Joseph Flipart and using the *opus sectile* technique.[4] Apparently much to the taste of the court of King Ferdinand VI of Spain, whose official painter Flipart was, these table tops were conceived as a trompe-l'œil, for the inlaid objects on them are represented exactly as one would expect to find them there in reality. But hard stone, obviously, is not well suited to creating an optical delusion and these works have a purely decorative and anecdotal value.

With the table tops of Flipart, one finds that trompe-l'œil, when forming part of a piece of furniture, can answer to quite different principles of design. The objects represented, instead of standing out from a vertical surface to which they are *fixed*, can be

△ René Dubois (1737-1799):
Detail of a Louis XVI Writing Table with Monochrome Painting in Trompe-l'œil, stamped "J. Dubois." Painted wood.

Charles-Joseph Flipart (1721-1797):
Inlaid Marble Table Top, 1760-1770.
Marble and hard stones.

Louis Léopold Boilly (1761-1845):
Trompe-l'œil Painting on the Top
of an Empire Pedestal Table,
1808-1814. Painted wood.

gathered together on a horizontal surface on which they are *laid down*. [5] Such is the meaning and purpose of a whole series of trompe-l'œil pieces which must originally have been table tops. As we see them today, detached from their support and hung on the wall, they are incongruous, because the objects represented, not being fixed, seem on the verge of giving way to the pull of gravity and falling to the floor. [6]

The top of an Empire pedestal table decorated by Boilly with a horizontal trompe-l'œil painting has come down to us in its original setting. [7] A masterpiece of pictorial skill, it represents some *works of art* in different media and some folded letters, but also a broken pane of glass, several coins and a magnifying glass. These unusually deceptive elements, which Boilly depicted repeatedly in his paintings, earned him a great success at the Paris Salons of the period.

firescreens

When the winter months were over and no fire was needed, the fireplace was always screened off with a panel.[8] Though of strictly practical use, these firescreens were also decorated in the style of the period. In the seventeenth century they began to be made of canvas mounted on a frame shaped to fit the hearth opening.[9] A century later they took the form of a trompe-l'œil painting. More than any other picture, these paintings made to measure had to harmonize with the home of the person who ordered them, reflecting his particular reality and style of life.

Long neglected and damaged by use, these firescreens were mutilated and cut down to a rectangle in order to turn them into conventional *still lifes* which in this form could be hung up at eye level.[10] Nevertheless they are readily recognizable as trompe-l'œil firescreens owing to their peculiar iconography and design. The unusual downward point of view uncovers a vase of flowers, a pet, small pieces of furniture or objects in disorder, which have temporarily been put away on the brick or stone floor of the fireplace emptied of its fire.

With their strong foreground lighting, their dark mysterious background, and above all their intimation of an interrupted activity, of a human presence that was there but a moment before, the firescreens of Chardin and Oudry[11] are masterpieces of trompe-l'œil and still life painting.

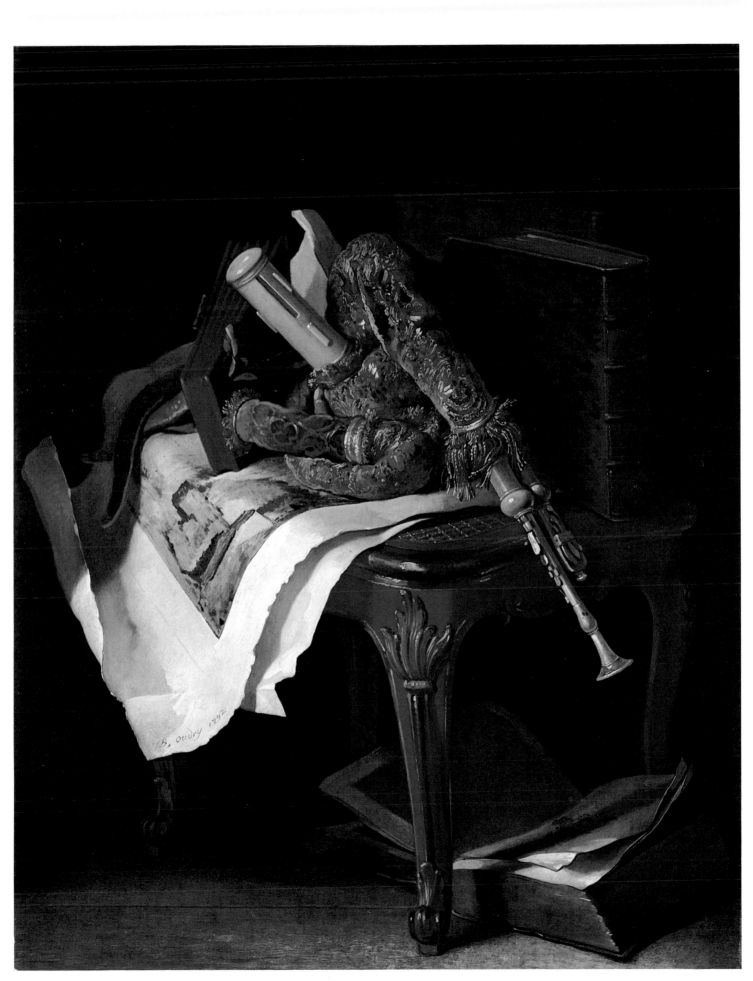

In turning to the cut-out the trompe-l'œil artist took a further step in his quest for a three-dimensional reality. Rejecting the background of the picture and the restrictive frame of the bordering rectangle, he proceeded to give the work the very shape of the reality he intended to represent. As we have already noted, Gijsbrechts probably made the painter's *mahlstick* *stand out* from the panel serving as background for his *Studio Wall with Vanitas*.[12] Going further, he gave a painted cut-out easel a potential mobility by detaching it completely from the wall. This offered a pretext for representing one of his still lifes, a picture lying face down on the floor, and a miniature portrait of his client.[13]

the painted cut-out

This device was apparently much appreciated and the idea was taken over by other painters.[14] Fifty years later Antonio Forbera placed on a cut-out easel the tools of the painter's craft, together with the inevitable canvas seen from the back and some prints by Perelle and Le Clerc. The most prominent place, however, is given to a copy of Poussin's *Empire of Flora*, whose clumsy brushwork is obviously deliberate. More skilful is the red chalk drawing of the same picture, placed above it, which must have served as the model for it. This ingenious trompe-l'œil evokes not only several levels of reality, but also several artistic personalities. Into his patron's house Forbera thus introduced a glimpse of a studio that was not his own, but rather that of an indifferent copyist. He only reveals himself to the spectator when the subterfuge is seen through, and then he asserts his personality as that of the talented artist who has stood aloof in order to execute a trompe-l'œil of high quality.

Charles de Brosses has left a revealing account of his sight of this cut-out *Easel*.[15] It is interesting to note the reaction of this cultivated literary man and connoisseur. De Brosses was taken in by the picture and resolved to test the reality of what he saw before him. Not only did he "finger" it, but moistening his handkerchief he tried to wipe out the drawing, which he thought was done in pencil. He was so pleased with the painting that he wished to purchase it; he was prepared, that is, to live with it. One is still prompted to wonder and admiration by this unusual piece of trompe-l'œil.

During the eighteenth century the movable object sometimes assumed the effigy of the masters of the house or their servants.[16] These human silhouettes undoubtedly originated in the Renaissance theatre, where they replaced the extras. They also had their place in the fun-loving tradition of the seventeenth-century Dutch painters. Well placed and cunningly lighted, such cut-outs could produce the desired effect. Today, however, the spectator may experience some difficulty in accepting the painted cut-out as a serious device, for with it we reach those shifting, ill-defined limits where trompe-l'œil passes over from the domain of art to that of the practical joke.

△ Anonymous:
Dummy Board (Silent Companion),
c. 1603-1625.
Painted wooden cut-out.

▷ Antonio Forbera (active
late 17th century):
Painter's Easel, 1686.
Oil on canvas cut-out.

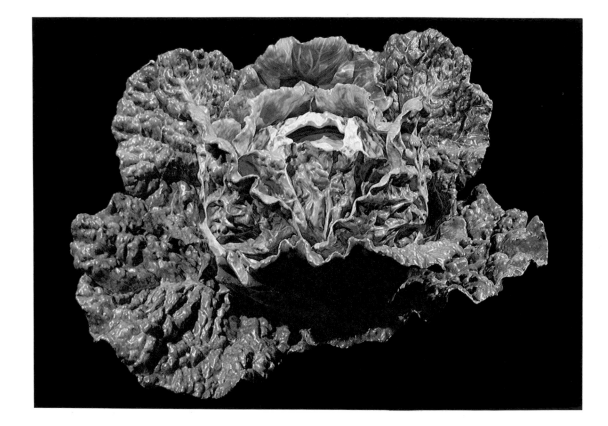

In the sixteenth century Bernard Palissy peopled his gardens with terracotta reptiles "enamelled so closely from nature that live lizards and snakes would often come and admire them."[17] Making the most of his technical discoveries, Palissy created faience wares ornamented with animals, vegetables and insects in relief. Stemming from the creative imagination of an age that was fascinated by visual ambiguity, they were considered as objects of art and found their place in the Cabinets of Curiosities.

When, later on, they were relieved of the improbable presence of unedible animals, these dishes and bowls became very popular wares and have continued to be made by potters down to the present day. The factitious reality of these essentially ornamental pieces can deceive no one; they are in fact sham objects.

Doubly deceptive, the earthenware soup-tureens in the form of a cabbage or lettuce are often disconcerting in their perfection. Not only does the colour glaze simulate plant life, but the apparently compact volume conceals the hollow structure of the vessel. Here the trompe-l'œil becomes a utility object.

the sham object

Trompe-l'œil or sculpture? The sham objects of Christian Renonciat transcend any definition. They are made of a material—wood—which the artist does not attempt to conceal, but which he transforms by a mutation that casts a spell over the senses. The material is no longer subordinated to the representation of the object; it is, rather, as Roger Caillois says, "the simulated (and contradictory) object which serves to bring out and so to represent and make us see the material of which it is made and thereby reveal it, for here the material is the subject of the work."[18]

◁ Strasbourg ware in the form of a cabbage. 18th century.

Christian Renonciat (1947):
Cotton and Feather, 1979.
Carving in American pinewood.

8

The sham trompe-l'œil

In the light of this survey of the various types of trompe-l'œil, a certain idiom becomes recognizable at first glance. It is an idiom which, in the end, can be dangerously akin to a recipe. Nevertheless the trompe-l'œil does not lend itself to a hasty examination, and a careful scrutiny often reveals unsuspected subtleties.

△ Sebastiano Lazzari (?-c. 1770):
Trompe-l'œil, 1756.
Oil on canvas.

◁ Edward Collier (1640-after 1706):
Still Life with Papers,
Books and Letter Rack.
Oil on canvas.

the quotation

Disorder, overlapping papers, books, letter racks, a picture within the picture, an indefinite background, a curtain—here is a familiar vocabulary. And yet we are in the presence neither of a trompe-l'œil nor of a conventional still life. Edward Collier's picture is obviously the reminiscence of a trompe-l'œil, a quotation made by an artist who practised this art form, addressing himself to a public that was familiar with it.

The painter thus attempts to make real and actual a cultural moment of great importance for the Protestant milieu in which he moved. This is his powerful evocation of a past in which Melanchthon, the master theologian, dominated the learning and the faith of his contemporaries. [1]

At first sight one notes that the picture of Sebastiano Lazzari is divided into two parts by a horizontal line. [2] In the foreground there is a still life standing on a table, outlined against a panelled background on which are laid out the elements of a classic trompe-l'œil. This division is certainly deliberate, for the way of treating textures and the intensity of the contrasts set the two parts of the picture in opposition. One is tempted to suppose that this, once again, is the *quotation* of a trompe-l'œil. But a change of focal distance leads the eye into the immediate foreground, to a piece of paper placed in front of the table and cut off by the edge of the picture. Its purpose is clear at once, for it removes the whole content of the representation to another level of reality. This picture calls for presentation in a frame into which the piece of paper may be slipped. It thus becomes the real *trompe-l'œil* of a *work of art* which in turn contains a *quotation* from a trompe-l'œil.

Pleasing to the eye, stimulating to the mind, the trompe-l'œil painting may also become a charade.

the knowing eye

By respecting the rules of the game, the trompe-l'œil painting can make the spectator believe that it replaces a certain reality.

The imagination of artists has created other works which conceal their reality under deceptive appearances. At first sight the knowing spectator is made aware of that hidden aspect by a deliberate response. Such works have only a formal connection with trompe-l'œil.

the peepshow

It is always difficult and risky to establish a causal relation between an economic context and the production of works of art. There is good reason, nevertheless, to suggest that the interest which Dutch artists of the seventeenth century took in optical problems was connected with the discovery of new instruments prompted by Dutch seafaring ventures of that day.[3] In view of the new conception of the picture space characteristic of the school of Rembrandt, one cannot help wondering whether the artists arising from that school, like Hoogstraten, Fabritius and above all Vermeer, did not resort to the *camera obscura* to obtain their extraordinary effects of light and depth.[4]

The peepshow box, of which only a few examples have survived, tangibly illustrates the interaction between the optical device and the representation of space. The one made by Carel Fabritius appears to be the earliest of the series. It was clearly of considerable interest to contemporaries, for as early as 1690 we find it in the *Kunstkammer* of the king of Denmark.[5] This perspective box looks like a small cabinet, and the inside walls are painted in distorting perspective to suggest the nave of a Protestant church. Receiving light from a rectangular aperture on the top, the painting is designed to be seen through a peephole on the right side of the central panel.

Viewing the painting in this way, isolated from the outside world, one gets a powerful sense of three-dimensional space, in which (as Hoogstraten wrote), "if it is painted with skill... a figure no bigger than a finger appears life-size."[6] Monocular vision from a fixed distance corrects the distortion and attenuates the distinction between surface and volume. At the same time, the walls of the box limit the vision on both sides, so lending a total credibility to the spatial cube. A curiosity rather than a work of art, the peepshow box shows with almost caricatural acuteness the limitations of the perspective construction, which only becomes perfect when the eye submits to constraints out of keeping with the physiology of vision.

In this artificial setting the trompe-l'œil painted on the exterior of Fabritius' peepshow box is perceived as a naïve but restful image, one reflecting an accessible reality.

anamorphosis

Probably the creation of Leonardo da Vinci,[7] anamorphosis stands at the opposite pole from trompe-l'œil. It gives the illusion of a non-reality, of a world which has no coherent form and no meaning. In its technique it is an extrapolation of perspective methods in the direction in which the results are farthest removed from the representation of reality. To rectify the distortion, the spectator has to stand at a very definite viewpoint or employ a suitable optical instrument.

On the other hand, the *Descent from the Cross* after Rubens becomes legible only if seen through a correcting cylindrical mirror placed in the centre of the chaotic image of the anamorphosis.

Arising from the geometric experiments of certain perspective artists of the Renaissance, anamorphosis began as a pseudo-scientific exercise with occult connotations; by the eighteenth century it had become a mere amusement or stunt.[8] When employed to illustrate the Vanitas theme, it did so in a manner diametrically opposed to trompe-l'œil. The latter aroused a moralizing train of thought by the reality of the symbolic objects represented, while anamorphosis unmistakably affirms the uncertainty of appearances. It might serve to illustrate Plato, for whom the work of art is a phantom of reality, just as well as Descartes, who extends his doubt over the whole of the world as perceived by the senses.

Trompe-l'œil is an affirmation of reality, anamorphosis a denial of it.

Flemish School (first
half of the 17th century):
Descent from the Cross, after Rubens.
Cylindrical anamorphosis.

The fortune of trompe-l'œil

If it is accepted that each cultural period creates its own climate of opinion, its own frame of mind and range of expectations, then the evolution of art is seen as a series of successive shocks produced by works which do not answer to the established norm. [1] In this case trompe-l'œil is an exception, for the reality of objects has changed little and its abiding purpose is to render that reality. Its fortune depends less on happy accidents or stylistic changes [2] than on the way the spectator makes contact with the work and accepts its content. It is perhaps for this reason that one can so readily compare works which are separated by centuries but which result from the same approach, the same visual or conceptual motivation.

Through its many facets, trompe-l'œil has always made its intention perfectly clear. Its express purpose is to mystify, to transcend and replace the illusion of reality by its certainty. In his race with reality, the trompe-l'œil painter has been led to respect certain rules and to use a vocabulary which has forced itself upon him as the one best suited to his purpose.

Trompe-l'œil at its most flawless, when carried through with unswerving logic, should achieve a total integration with its environment and so pass unnoticed. If the setting of the picture lends itself to the game, the situation is possible and the history of art provides examples of this. Sometimes, to catch the eye, trompe-l'œil provokes the spectator's attention by some incongruous details and compels him to become aware of it.

Even though trompe-l'œil is meant to deceive and in some cases very nearly succeeds, it is not always accepted at once as a reality. At first sight the image comes as a surprise. By turns it inspires doubt and certainty in a continual readjustment of the gaze. The puzzled viewer is torn between the message of his eyes and the message of his brain. The mind may already know the right answer, and yet the spectator's reaction is to abandon his receptive passiveness and act in order to test what he sees.

A "relation of uncertainty" [3] is thus created between the image and the viewer, which makes the situation ambiguous and, in the end, infinitely pleasant.

The game may be a familiar one for the knowing public who is aware of similar past experiences. Then the very fact of knowing that the picture was designed to arouse doubt enriches the contact with it.

When, at a subsequent moment, the mystification becomes certain and unmistakable, is the picture to be rejected? It is at this point that one begins to realize what is meant by the strange and well-defined world of trompe-l'œil. A world without history or features, with no horizon or depth, in which the arts exchange their means of expression; peopled with salient and aggressive objects, it bathes in a lunar light coming out of nowhere. Chosen and organized according to the ritual dictated by *the rules of the*

game, the repertory of trompe-l'œil painting is made up of obsessive elements, it represents a reality immobilized by nails, held in the grip of death, corroded by time, glimpsed through half-open doors or undrawn curtains, containing messages that are sometimes unreadable, allusions that are often misunderstood, and a disorder of seemingly familiar and yet remote objects.

The artist has organized this vocabulary in such a way as to make up a language whose meaning reflects the climate peculiar to himself. Each image in trompe-l'œil thus amounts to a position taken up by its creator with respect to the reality which he represents; it is also, very often, an involuntary token of his personality and preoccupations.

The spectator contemporary with the painter, to whom the picture was initially addressed, who lived in the same surroundings and shared the same heritage of values, was able to interpret the picture directly, on the lines laid down by the artist. Thus at the time of their creation the trompe-l'œil paintings were seen by turns as spiritual messages or moral lessons, as curiosities or occult manifestations of some peculiar mysticism. Later on, they were drained of their emblematic content and became a *jeu d'esprit* but also a nostalgic reminder of the past. In present-day art the reality they so pointedly impose is sometimes that of a dreamworld [4] which one despairs of ever attaining. The trompe-l'œil picture is an image whose conceptual content has continually changed in spite of its iconography and its limited repertory.

When a lapse of time intervenes between the creation and reception of the work, the interpretation of a trompe-l'œil may become complex, for it is a mirror full of ambiguous reflections, also giving back both the image of the spectator and the image of his world with its own fancies and peculiar truths. [5]
Visually fascinating, now moralizing, now indiscreet, dissenting or ironical, trompe-l'œil remains a strange and provocative art rich in implications.

Richard Haas (1936):
Crossroads Building, Times Square,
New York City.
Painted façade, 1980.

Notes and references

Foreword (page 6)

[1] *The Elder Pliny's Chapters on the History of Art.*, translated by Katharine Jex-Blake, Chicago, 1976, p. 10.

[2] Like all definitions laid down in the field of the so-called human sciences, those given here do not pretend to be universally valid; they are meant to serve, coherently it is hoped, only for the purposes of this book.

[3] Gombrich has shown how important the factors of "expectation" and "education" are in our acceptance and interpretation of illusion.
See E. H. Gombrich, *Art and Illusion, A Study in the Psychology of Pictorial Representation*, New York-London, 1960; and R. L. Gregory and E. H. Gombrich, *Illusion in Nature and Art*, New York-London, 1973.

[4] Sandström has formulated a system of "levels of unreality" which he applies to the study of illusionist wall painting.
See Sven Sandström, *Levels of Unreality*, Uppsala, 1963.

[5] Many artists have recorded their express intention to deceive and their pleasure when they succeed.
See Martin Battersby, *Trompe-l'œil: The Eye Deceived*, London, 1974.

Chapter 1 (page 9)

[1] Erwin Panofsky, *Early Netherlandish Painting*, New York, 1971, p. 131.

[2] There can be no question that the pottery depicted was the image of a reality. The large pharmacy jar *(albarello)*, for example, is recognizable as a ware that was made at Manises in Spain from 1430 on.

[3] Horace Walpole, *Anecdotes of Painting in England*, 1762, tells the same story about a fly painted by Holbein in 1526. Cited in Jurgis Baltrusaitis, *Anamorphoses*, Paris, 1969.

[4] Another way of placing the title in a fore-stage of the picture, outside its context and *in trompe-l'œil*, is to inscribe it on the *frame* (Piero di Cosimo, *Simonetta Vespucci*, Musée Condé, Chantilly) or else to engrave it on a stone parapet (Jan van Eyck, *Leal Souvenir*, National Gallery, London).

[5] D'Otrange Mastai rightly speaks of a real "papyromania." See M. L. d'Otrange Mastai, *Illusion in Art. Trompe l'œil: A History of Pictorial Illusionism*, New York, 1975, and London, 1976, p. 208.

Chapter 2 (page 14)

[1] See Erwin Panofsky, "Die Perspektive als symbolische Form," *Vorträge der Bibliothek Warburg*, 1924-1925, and Robert Klein, *La Forme et l'Intelligible*, Paris, 1970.

[2] See Anthony Blunt, "Illusionist Decoration in Central Italian Painting of the Renaissance," *Journal of the Royal Society of Art*, 1959, p. 321.

[3] No easel paintings have come down to us from Antiquity, but their existence is vouched for by literary descriptions and some of the Pompeii frescoes.

[4] This privileged spectator is certainly the master of the house and the point of view might correspond to the place he occupied either at table or during receptions.
See the reference cited in note 2 above.

[5] For a discussion of painted architecture, see André Chastel, *Le Grand Atelier d'Italie, 1460-1500*, Paris, 1965; English translation, *Studios and Styles of the Italian Renaissance*, London-New York, 1966.

[6] The model which the donor carries in the scene of the *Last Judgment* represents the chapel with a transept.

[7] See Charles de Tolnay, "Notes sur les origines de la nature morte," *Revue des Arts*, 1953, p. 66, and "Postilla sulle origini della natura morta moderna," *Rivista d'Arte*, No. 36, 1961-1962, p. 3.

[8] These niches have given rise to controversial discussions concerning the origin of the still life.
See Charles Sterling, *La Nature Morte de l'Antiquité à nos Jours*, Paris, 1959 (English translation, *Still Life from Antiquity to the Present Time*, New York, 1959); E. H. Gombrich, *Meditations on a Hobby Horse*, London-New York, 1978; Ingvar Bergström, *Dutch Still-Life Painting in the Seventeenth Century*, London, 1956.

[9] This type of niche must have been widespread in the fifteenth century, for we find it both in the luxurious apartments of the Vatican (Mantegna and Pinturicchio) and in the modest chapel of a castle in the Val d'Aosta (Castello di Fenis). These wall paintings were probably the first to be overpainted by later decorations.

[10] See E. H. Gombrich, *Meditations on a Hobby Horse*, London-New York, 1978, p. 103.

[11] The frescoes in the Collegiate church of Castiglione Olona were executed by Masolino, Paolo Schiavo and Vecchietta.

[12] It was not until a quarter of a century later that Pinturicchio (Cappella Baglioni at Spello) and Perugino (Collegio del Cambio at Perugia) painted their self-portraits *in trompe-l'œil* on simulated panels hanging on the walls represented in their frescoes.

[13] The pilasters give rhythm to the mosaic zones and the whole is crowned by a *velarium* with a pierced centre.

[14] See Ingrid Sjöstrom, *Quadratura: Studies in Italian Ceiling Painting*, Stockholm, 1978.

[15] For an analysis of the decorative systems with simulated architecture, see Catherine Dumont, *Francesco Salviati au Palais Sacchetti de Rome et la décoration murale italienne (1520-1560)*, Institut Suisse, Rome, 1973. For the Baroque period, see M. C. Gloton, *Trompe-l'œil et décor plafonnant dans les églises romaines de l'âge baroque*, Rome, 1965.

[16] Giulio Romano, Sala dei Giganti, Palazzo del Te, Mantua.

[17] As precursors we may mention the *velum* representing the Feast of the Gods in the Loggia of Psyche (Farnesina, Rome) and the simulated tapestries in the Sala di Costantino (Vatican) by Raphael; later on, the frescoes of Domenichino, Zucchi, etc.
See C. Dumont, reference cited in note 15 above, and U. Reinhart, "La tapisserie feinte. Un genre de décoration du maniérisme romain du XVIe siècle," *Gazette des Beaux-Arts*, No. 84, 1974, p. 285.

[18] For the attribution of these Vatican frescoes, see John Shearman, in *Festschrift für Walter Friedländer zum 90. Geburtstag*, Berlin, 1965.

[19] See the catalogue of the exhibition *La Grisaille*, Palais de Tokyo, Paris, 1980.

[20] See G. and C. Thiem, *Toskanische Fassaden-Dekoration in Sgraffito und Fresko*, Munich, 1964.

[21] See Alessandro Marabottini, *Polidoro da Caravaggio*, Rome, 1969.

Chapter 3 (page 34)

[1] For a study of flower still lifes, see Ingvar Bergström, *Dutch Still-Life Painting*, London, 1956.

[2] The sense of depth is given by the adjustment of the two eyes looking at objects placed at different distances (parallax effect) and by the change in the relative positions of these objects when the spectator moves in front of them. These two factors disappear when the eyes look at the plane surface of a picture. For the trompe-l'œil to bring off its effect, the field represented must be as shallow as possible.
Thus the most "effective" trompe-l'œil pictures were those representing the *Five Dollar Bill* by N. A. Brooks (1890, Private Collection) and the postage stamp in *Which is Which?* by J. D. Chalfant (1890, Private Collection); the painted stamp of the latter is better preserved than the real one beside it. Here one may wonder at what point the painter's work ends and the forger's begins.

[3] Martin Battersby, a contemporary English painter, has explained the procedures he uses in order to deceive the spectator successfully.
See his book, *Trompe-l'œil: The Eye Deceived*, London, 1974.

[4] See Alberto Veca in the catalogue of the exhibition *Inganno & Realtà. Trompe l'œil in Europa XVI-XVIII secoli*, Galleria Lorenzelli, Bergamo, 1980, p. 100.

Chapter 4 (page 38)

[1] "Mors quam amara est memoria tua homini injusto..." The text comes from *Ecclesiasticus*, chapter XLI, and the word "injusto" was added by the scribe to the Vulgate text.
See Edouard Michel, *Musée National du Louvre, Catalogue Raisonné des Peintures du Moyen Age, de la Renaissance et des Temps Modernes. Peintures Flamandes du XVe-XVIe siècle*, Paris, 1953, p. 275.

[2] See Paul Leprieur, "Un triptyque de Roger de la Pasture," *Gazette des Beaux-Arts*, 1913, II, p. 257. Quoted in E. Michel, reference cited in note 1 above.

[3] Jan van Eyck had used the same objects, in a like setting, but integrated into the panel representing the Annunciation on the reverse of the *Polyptych of the Mystical Lamb* in St Bavo's Cathedral, Ghent.

[4] For symbolism in the painting of the fifteenth and sixteenth centuries, see Ingvar Bergström, "Disguised

Symbolism in 'Madonna' Pictures and Still-Life," *The Burlington Magazine*, 97, 1955.

Erwin Panofsky, *Early Netherlandish Painting*, New York, 1971, p. 131.

[5] Luther explained as follows the words "our daily bread" in the Lord's Prayer: "All that belongs to the maintenance of the body and the bare necessities of life, such as food and drink, clothes, house and home, cattle, furniture, money, a good wife, well-behaved children... and many other such things." Quoted in Ingvar Bergström, *Dutch Still-Life Painting*, London, 1956, pp. 1-2.

[6] The Vanitas theme has recently been analysed by Alberto Veca, catalogue of the exhibition *Vanitas*, Galleria Lorenzelli, Bergamo, 1981.

Christian Klemm in the catalogue of the exhibition *Stilleben in Europa*, Münster and Baden-Baden, 1979-1980, p. 140.

[7] These two companion pieces were attributed by Michel Faré to Houasse thanks to the objects and statues represented, which reappear in another, signed picture (Royal Palace, Madrid).

Michel and Fabrice Faré, *La vie silencieuse en France. La nature morte au XVIIIe siècle*, Fribourg (Switzerland), 1976, p. 36.

Bergström's view is that the trompe-l'œil niches simulating the wall might have been inserted into the wall of the room.

Ingvar Bergström, catalogue of the exhibition *Natura in Posa*, Galleria Lorenzelli, Bergamo, 1971.

One may also note the elegant solution of the collector who, in the absence of a marble wall, evokes its existence by a trompe-l'œil frame which imitates its texture.

[8] For the symbolism of the mirror and the horse, see Edgar Wind, *Pagan Mysteries in the Renaissance*, London, 1958, p. 125.

Cesare Ripa, *Iconologia* (1613), Hildesheim-New York, 1970, p. 479.

Achille Bocchi, *Symbolicarum Quaestionum de Universo Genere... libri quinque*, Bologna, 1574; London, 1979 (Symb. CXVII and LXV).

[9] The central panel of the Aix altarpiece is in the Church of the Madeleine, Aix-en-Provence. The wing representing Jeremiah, surmounted by a still life in trompe-l'œil, is in the Musées Royaux des Beaux-Arts, Brussels. The other wing, representing Isaiah, has been separated from its still life and is in the Museum Boymans-van Beuningen, Rotterdam.

[10] See Alberto Veca, exhibition catalogue *Vanitas*, Galleria Lorenzelli, Bergamo, 1981.

[11] See Charles Sterling, *La Nature Morte de l'Antiquité à nos Jours*, Paris, 1959, p. 25.

[12] Hainz's picture was ordered by King Christian IV of Denmark, whose name is engraved on one of the crystal goblets and whose portrait can be seen in the painting. Some of the objects depicted here are still in the royal Danish collections.

See Liselotte Möller, "Georg Hintz' Kunstschrank-Bilder und der Meister der grossen Elfenbeinpokale," *Jahrbuch der Hamburger Kunstsammlung*, Vol. 8, 1963, p. 64.

[13] For a study of the representation of collections in still life pictures, see Gisela Luther, catalogue of the exhibition *Stilleben in Europa*, Münster and Baden-Baden, 1979-1980, p. 88.

[14] Valette-Penot's picture is one of a group of three trompe-l'œil paintings (Nos. 631-633 in M. and F. Faré, *La vie silencieuse en France*, Fribourg, 1976); the other two were originally the front and back of a single panel. M. Ramade, Curator of the Musée des Beaux-Arts, Rennes, has orally confirmed the close connection between the real source of light and Valette-Penot's cabinet. Indeed, the cross-barred windows reflected in the glass objects (and in their shadows) are the exact replica of those in the Hôtel de Robien, Rennes, home of the collector who ordered the picture. The name and address of Mademoiselle de Robien figure in one of the paintings (Faré, No. 632) and some of the objects and works of art represented are now in the Rennes museum. Jean Valette-Penot's three trompe-l'œil paintings therefore seem *exemplary* in their reflection of the actual life-setting and personality of those for whom they were made.

For a different opinion, see Joseph Lammers, catalogue of the exhibition *Stilleben in Europa*, Münster and Baden-Baden, 1979-1980, p. 490.

[15] See also Charles Sterling, catalogue of the exhibition *La Nature Morte de l'Antiquité à nos Jours*, Orangerie, Paris, 1952, and Giuseppe Delogu, *Natura morta italiana*, Bergamo, 1962, p. 66.

[16] See André Chastel, *Fables, Figures, Formes*, Paris, 1978, Vol. 1, p. 317.

[17] Charles Sterling, *La Nature Morte*, Paris, 1959; E. H. Gombrich, *Meditations on a Hobby Horse*, London-New York, 1978; Ingvar Bergström, *Dutch Still-Life Painting*, London, 1956.

[18] See Wolfgang Liebenwein, *Studiolo. Die Entstehung eines Raumtyps und seine Entwicklung bis 1600*, Berlin, 1977.

[19] In analysing Holbein's *Ambassadors* (National Gallery, London), Baltrusaitis has explained the evolution of the mentality that led from the *Vanitas* picture as *memento mori* to its subsequent associations with the arts, the sciences, faith, and death.

Jurgis Baltrusaitis, *Anamorphoses*, Paris, 1969.

[20] One must try to forget the panels (designed though they were by masters like Botticelli) which, by their re-presentation of allegorical figures or landscapes, disturb the sense of a pseudo-reality.

[21] These *intarsie* are still being made in the Jansen workshops, Paris.

[22] The collector in question may possibly have been a member of the Medici family.

Chapter 5 (page 54)

[1] The success of this procedure was noted in a text dated 1463, referring to a picture by Simon Marmion. It was judged "singular in the drapery, a salience of flat painting so that anyone not looking at it closely would swear it to be white stone."

Quoted in D. Coekelberghs, "Les grisailles de Van Eyck," *Gazette des Beaux-Arts*, 1968, p. 79.

[2] The grisailles represented on the reverse of polyptychs followed an interesting evolution. Starting from the trompe-l'œil of a statue, they then represented hybrids in movement (Hugo van der Goes, *Portinari Altarpiece*, Uffizi, Florence) and at the end of the sixteenth century became illusionist paintings in grey monochrome.
See P. Philippot, "Les grisailles et les 'degrés de réalité' de l'image dans les peintures flamandes du XVe et XVIe siècles," *Bulletin des Musées Royaux des Beaux-Arts de Belgique*, fasc. 4, 1966, p. 225.

[3] See Johan Huizinga, *L'automne du moyen âge*, Paris, 1975, p. 319; in English, *The Waning of the Middle Ages*, London, 1948.

[4] Panofsky has emphasized the direct contact that existed in the fifteenth century between the painter and the sculptor. Indeed, even the greatest Flemish masters were expected to colour statues. They accordingly had the opportunity of seeing them, as Panofsky puts it, "in the nude" and appreciating the play of light on pure forms. In their illusionistic representation of sculpture in grey or "stone colour," the painters—according to Panofsky—acted as pioneers and educated both public and sculptors to appreciate uncoloured statues.
See Erwin Panofsky, *Early Netherlandish Painting*, New York, 1971, p. 162.
Smith, on the other hand, suggests that the grisailles were associated with the period of Lent, for which the *Parement de Narbonne* (Louvre, Paris) is known to have been executed (in monochrome). Lent was also the period during which, in churches, only the figures of saints and the *Annunciations* remained undraped.
See M.T. Smith, "The Use of Grisaille as Lenten Observance," *Marsyas*, Vol. VIII, 1957-1959, p. 43.
Nevertheless, considering the richness and diversity of the material available, it seems improbable that the monochrome grey should have always been akin to penitence. It is also difficult to imagine that important patrons would accept images which were—according to Panofsky—the trompe-l'œil of an *unfinished* object. It seems more likely that only wood or stone statuary was polychrome and that the grisailles were the replica of precious and rare alabaster or marble pieces which have, possibly, never been coloured.
The author is grateful to Professor F. Deuchler who suggested this possibility.

[5] Raphael, *The Small Holy Family*, 1518-1519, Louvre, Paris.

[6] See the catalogues of the exhibitions *Gray is the Color*, Rice Museum, Houston, Texas, 1974, and *La Grisaille*, Palais de Tokyo, Paris, 1980.

[7] In spite of its astonishing verisimilitude, the simulated bas-relief of Nicolas-Guy Brenet does not appear to be the replica of any particular ancient relief, but rather the outcome of a visual synthesis of works which the artist had seen in Rome.
See M.-F. Pérez, *Bulletin de la Société de l'Histoire de l'Art français*, Paris, 1974, p. 199.

[8] Though highly critical of trompe-l'œil, Diderot yielded to the ones executed by artists whom he admired.
Thus, of Oudry, he writes: "Do you remember two bas-reliefs painted by Oudry to which one put one's hand? The hand touched a plane surface; and the eye, still allured, saw a relief; so that one might have asked the philosopher which of the two senses whose testimonies contradicted each other was mendacious?" Diderot, *Salons de 1759, 1761, 1763*, edited by Jean Seznec, reprinted in Collection Images et Idées, p. 84.
Referring again to Oudry: "Oudry's bas-reliefs, placed among the sculptures, were so true that only by touch could the eye be undeceived." Diderot, *Salons*, Vol. III, 1767, edited by Jean Seznec and Jean Adhémar, Oxford, 1967, p. 203.
This testimony is doubly interesting, for it confirms the fact that trompe-l'œil bas-reliefs were deliberately exhibited among the sculptures. See also note 17 below.
Of Chardin, Diderot writes: "The illusion here is of the greatest force and I have seen more than one person deceived by it." Diderot, *Salons*, Vol. IV, 1771, Oxford, 1967, p. 178.

[9] Gijsbrechts, the absolute master of trompe-l'œil, made countless representations of *pictures*. In Chapter 3 we have seen the simplest case, but perhaps the most refined: the Vanitas picture is presented unframed and a corner of the canvas is detached from the stretcher, curling up towards the spectator. In other cases the *canvas* is frayed and ill fastened to a wooden panel which serves as support. For further examples see Georges Marlier, "C.N. Gijsbrechts l'illusionniste," *Connaissance des Arts*, 1964, No. 145; Poul Gammelbo, *Dutch Still-Life Painting from the 16th to the 18th Centuries in Danish Collections*, Copenhagen-Amsterdam, 1960, and "Cornelis Norbertus Gijsbrechts og Franciscus Gijsbrechts," *Kunstmuseets Aarsskrift*, 39-42, 1952-1955, p. 25.

[10] Salmi points to the existence of a local tradition of trompe-l'œil representations of rolled-up and torn papers in manuscript illuminations.
See Mario Salmi, "Riflessioni sulla Civiltà figurativa di Ferrara nei suoi rapporti con Padova durante il primo Rinascimento," *Rivista d'Arte*, 1959, Vol. XXXIV, seria terza, Vol. IX, p. 35.

[11] Gerard Dou, *Self-Portrait*, 1645, Rijksmuseum, Amsterdam.
For a detailed analysis of the picture, see M. L. d'Otrange Mastai, *Illusion in Art*, New York, 1975, and London, 1976, p. 187.

[12] Rembrandt, *Holy Family*, 1646, Gemäldegalerie, Kassel.

[13] The *cartellino* bears the inscription "Verona" and "fatta nel monasterio Santo Angolo" (instead of Santo Angelo). Since the artist's name is Angolo, one cannot help wondering whether it is a coincidence or a play of *names* accompanying the play of images. The ambiguity remains.
See W. Stechow, *European and American Paintings and Sculpture in the Allen Memorial Art Museum*, Oberlin College, Oberlin, Ohio, 1967.

[14] Fabrizio Clerici, "The Grand Illusion," *Art News Annual*, 1954, p. 100.

[15] For other examples, see M. and F. Faré, *La vie silencieuse en France. La nature morte au XVIIIe siècle*, Fribourg, 1976, and M. and F. Faré, "Le trompe-l'œil dans la peinture française du XVIIIe siècle," *L'Œil*, No. 257, 1976, p. 2.

[16] This (unpublished) trompe-l'œil signed by Gresly enables us, thanks to the objects it contains, to reconsider the attribution of a large trompe-l'œil with pendant representing a library, shown in the exhibition *Inganno & Realtà*, Bergamo, 1980, as Nos. XXII and XXIII, and in the exhibition *Cristoforo Munari e la natura morta emiliana*, Parma, 1964, as Nos. 54 and 55. For in it we find the same print of *The Surgeon* and the same *Almanach du solitaire*, together with a print by Perelle (often represented by Gresly) and a treatise on painting in French.
The picture by the anonymous eighteenth-century Dutch master (in Martin Battersby, *Trompe-l'œil: The Eye Deceived*, London, 1974, p. 140) also needs to be reconsidered.
A study is currently being made.

[17] The problem of the *perfect* trompe-l'œil, whose subterfuge goes undiscovered and which, *de facto*, takes the place of reality, was already stated by a critic who saw a "bas-relief" by Chardin at the Salon of 1771:
Monsieur X.: "did not *see* the bas-reliefs, inasmuch as he took them for sculpture"...
Monsieur Y.: "was not fooled for—in spite of the Swiss guards—he touched the pictures."
Quoted in Diderot, *Salons*, Vol. IV, 1769-1771-1775-1781, edited by Jean Seznec, Oxford, 1967, p. 23.

[18] The existence of the goldsmith Guillaume Bert at Dunkerque is documented and works by him are known.

[19] See C. Burda, *Das Trompe l'œil in der holländischen Malerei des 17. Jahrhunderts*, Inaugural Dissertation, Munich, 1969, p. 70.

[20] See Alberto Veca, exhibition catalogue *Inganno & Realtà*, Galleria Lorenzelli, Bergamo, 1980, p. 190.

[21] Owing to this similarity of basic principles, the photographic reproduction of a painted perspective benefits from the monocular vision and privileged position of the motionless camera. Thus Cuchi White's photographs of simulated architecture make use of this privilege and fully succeed in evoking all the magic of a fiction which merges with reality.
See Georges Perec and Cuchi White, *L'œil ébloui*, Paris, 1981.

[22] Martin Battersby, *Trompe-l'œil: The Eye Deceived*, London, 1974, p. 21.

[23] Comparison of Braun's photograph with Harnett's picture *After the Hunt* (see Chapter 6) leaves no doubt that the American painter must have seen the photographer's work during a journey to Europe.
See Alfred Frankenstein, *The Reality of Appearance: The Trompe-l'œil Tradition in American Painting*, New York Graphic Society, Greenwich, Connecticut, 1970.

[24] See Georges Marlier, "C. N. Gijsbrechts l'illusionniste," *Connaissance des Arts*, 1964, No. 145.

[25] According to d'Otrange Mastai, the word "canvasback" (which is also the name of an American wild duck), appearing on Davis' picture, is an invitation to turn the canvas over and at the same time an ironical comment on trompe-l'œil pictures with *hunting trophies* showing animals with strange names.
See M. L. d'Otrange Mastai, *Illusion in Art*, New York, 1975, and London, 1976, p. 287.

[26] J. F. Peto, *Lincoln and the Phleger Stretcher*, 1898, The New Britain Museum of American Art, New Britain, Connecticut.

Chapter 6 (page 72)

[1] Both Giovanni Bellini and Carpaccio signed nearly all their pictures on *cartellini*. Each of these scraps of paper represented a stage in the technical search for the trompe-l'œil effect. Furthermore, in the *studiolo* of Carpaccio's St Augustine (in the *Vision of St Augustine*, San Giorgio degli Schiavoni, Venice), we find a multitude of objects so grouped and treated as to make them stand out from their pictorial setting. In the same cycle we observe a letter rack attached to a wall running parallel to the picture surface; it has no iconographical reason for being there, apart from serving as a spatial device which was meant to culminate (or had *already* culminated) in an independent trompe-l'œil. This *incorporated* letter rack is to be found on the left side of the Carpaccio panel representing *Christ Calling Matthew*.

[2] The cut-off stem of the lily on the recto and the cut-off cornice on the verso confirm the mutilation of the picture and might help to identify the missing part.

[3] The imitation of textures by painting was perhaps one of the first absolute successes of trompe-l'œil.
See S. de Plas, "L'art insolite du Trompe-l'Œil," *Jardin des Arts*, Vol. 197, 1971, p. 64, and A. Knoepfli, "Matériaux colorés factices," *Palette*, Vol. 34, 1970, p. 7.

[4] In almost all the trompe-l'œil pictures of J. F. Peto (a painter of the second American school of trompe-l'œil), one gets this sense of abandonment and destruction. According to his biographers, Peto went from setback to setback in his life as an artist and experienced to the full the hardships of poverty.
See also note 16 below.

[5] See Georges Marlier, "C. N. Gijsbrechts l'illusionniste," *Connaissance des Arts*, 1964, No. 145; Poul Gammelbo, *Dutch Still-Life Painting from the 16th to the 18th Centuries in Danish Collections*, Copenhagen-Amsterdam, 1960, and "Cornelis Norbertus Gijsbrechts og Franciscus Gijsbrechts," *Kunstmuseets Aarsskrift*, 39-42, 1952-1955.

[6] For the symbolism of objects in Vanitas pictures, see note 6, Chapter 4.

[7] The decorations given him by the Emperor Ferdinand III were a "chain of honour" and a medal. The episode is related by Hoogstraten in his book *Inleyding tot de Hooge Schoole der Schilderkonst*, Rotterdam, 1678, and by his pupil Arnold Houbraken in *De groote Schouburgh der nederlantsche Konstschilders en Schilderessen*, Amsterdam, 1718, cited in H. Veys, "Neuerwerbung," *Jahrbuch der Staatlichen Kunstsammlungen in Baden Württemberg*, Vol. 12, 1975, p. 282.

[8] The verses were written by Johann Wilhelm von Stubenberg.

[9] The two plays by Hoogstraten are *Dierijk en Dorothé*, The Hague, 1666, and *De Roomsche Paulina*, The Hague, 1660.

[10] From Hoogstraten's writings, the following passage may be quoted: "Apprentices set out playfully (on panels or walls) everyday objects in natural and cut-out colours, such as letters and combs. They find that it is easy to represent flat things on a flat ground. Yet honour can be won by deceiving princes and princesses... Fruit or flower still lifes serve moreover as practice in good taste and colour composition." Free translation of the passage quoted by Jochen Becker, catalogue of the exhibition *Stilleben in Europa*, Münster and Baden-Baden, 1980, p. 469.

[11] The still life *Ego sum pictor* figures in the inventory of paintings found in Doncre's house after his death and that of his wife. This, then, would be a case in which a trompe-l'œil representing a corner of the artist's studio is documented as having its place in the house of its maker, where it should logically be found.
See M. and F. Faré, *La vie silencieuse en France. La nature morte au XVIIIe siècle*, Fribourg, 1976, p. 331.

[12] The portrait of Charles I was already associated with a Vanitas only two years after his death (picture of Laurensz van der Vinne, Louvre, Paris). The engraved portrait of the king appears on a sheet of paper in another *Letter Rack* by Collier (Private Collection) and on a medallion in several others.

[13] The subject must have found (sixteen years after the Revolution) an interested public, for there exists another *Ordonnance du Roi* by the same painter, similarly torn (Private Collection).

[14] Jacopo de Barbari, *Partridge*, 1504, Alte Pinakothek, Munich. It was shown and discussed at the exhibition *La Nature Morte de l'Antiquité à nos Jours*, Paris, 1952.

[15] See "Louis XV, ses trophées de chasse," *Connaissance des Arts*, Vol. 188, 1967, p. 110.

[16] The first generation of American painters (the "colonialists") made its appearance after the Revolution of 1776. Generally self-taught, producing portraits in series, they seem to have discovered by themselves, remote from any tradition, the charms and rules of trompe-l'œil. Among them were Copley, Chandler and members of the Peale family.
Abandoned for half a century, the American trompe-l'œil enjoyed a second flowering between 1850 and 1900. By then, for some of these artists, contact with the European tradition had already been made. The names of John Frederick Peto, John Haberle and William Keane may be mentioned.
See M. L. d'Orange Mastai, *Illusion in Art*, New York, 1975, and London, 1976, p. 259, and Alfred Frankenstein, *The Reality of Appearance: The Trompe l'Œil Tradition in American Painting*, Greenwich, Connecticut, 1970.

[17] See A. P. de Mirimonde, "Les peintres flamands de trompe-l'œil et de nature morte au XVIIe siècle et les sujets de musique," *Jaarboek van het Koningklijk Museum voor Schone Kunsten*, Antwerp, 1971, p. 223.

Chapter 7 (page 86)

[1] See also the anonymous Flemish master's *Still Life in a Cupboard*, 1538 (page 44) and Crespi's *Shelves with Music Books*, 1710 (page 49), which were both cupboard doors.

[2] There exists a set of twelve panels imitating bronze which Martin van Heemskerck (1535) made to be inserted in the wainscoting of a room. These panels are now dispersed in several museums.
See the catalogue of the exhibition *Gray is the Color*, Rice Museum, Houston, Texas, 1974.

[3] Another piece of furniture (an escritoire or *bonheur-du-jour*) decorated in the same manner and stamped "J. Dubois" is in the Petit Palais, Paris.

[4] See Ferdinando Rossi, *Mosaics, A Survey of their History and Techniques*, London, 1970.

[5] Among the earliest known examples of table tops painted in trompe-l'œil is the *Holbein Table*, 1515, now attributed to Hans Herbst (Schweizerisches Landesmuseum, Zürich). Imitating slate and decorated with narrative scenes, it also contains a few objects painted in trompe-l'œil (spectacles, a pen, a seal).
See L. Wüthrich, *Hans Herbst, ein Basler Maler der Frührenaissance*, International Congress of the History of Art, Budapest, 1969, p. 771.

[6] The curious trompe-l'œil paintings on backed paper by Antonio Piaggio, Michele Bracci and Stefano Mulinari shown at the exhibition *Inganno & Realtà*, Bergamo, 1980, as well as the *Letter Racks* bearing the Nos. 272-275 in d'Otrange Mastai (*Illusion in Art*, London, 1976) were very probably table tops.
The table top bears Boilly's name and address, written on a piece of paper: "M. Boilly rue Meslée 12 à Paris."

[7] According to an unverified tradition, this (unpublished) pedestal table belonged to Napoleon (communication from the Curator of the Lille Museum).

[8] The fireplace represented in Rogier van der Weyden's *Annunciation* (Chapter I) is closed off by a simple wooden panel.

[9] See also M. G. de Lastic Saint-Jal, "Les devants de cheminée," *Connaissance des Arts*, 39, May 1955, p. 26.

[10] Among the still lifes illustrated in Michel Faré, *La nature morte en France. Son histoire et son évolution du XVIIe au XXe siècle*, Geneva, 1962, Nos. XI, 137, 338, 339, 352 and 374 are very probably firescreens.

[11] Oudry's lacquered stool was painted for Watelet (a Receveur des Finances) and exhibited at the Salon of 1742 before being handed over to him.

[12] See page 66.

[13] The miniature portrait is that of King Christian V of Denmark; the painted cut-out by Gijsbrechts, made in 1670, is in the Statens Museum for Kunst, Copenhagen.

[14] The painted cut-outs by Munari figuring in the exhibition *Cristoforo Munari e la natura morta emiliana*, Parma, 1964, under Nos. 51-53, indicate the interest shown in Italy for the cut-outs of Gijsbrechts.

[15] Charles de Brosses (1709-1777), magistrate, politician, scholar, archaeologist, historian, and president of the parliament of Burgundy, left many writings. His impressions of the cut-out easel of Antonio Forbera (Antoine Fort-Bras) are to be found in his *Lettres familières sur l'Italie*, written in 1739-1740 and published

by Yvonne Bezard, Paris, 1931, p. 15: "I perceived all this, both from a distance and from close at hand, without finding anything which made it worthwhile to pause over it. But my surprise was unmatched when, in trying to take up the drawing, I found that it was not real and that the whole was but a single picture entirely painted in oils. I moistened my handkerchief and passed it over the drawing, unable to convince myself that it was not drawn in pencil. The imprint of the plate mark on the paper of the two prints, the difference in texture between the papers, the character of the two prints, the canvas threads of the overturned picture, the holes and wood of the easel, all this is so admirable... I would gladly have given two hundred louis for it... The singular thing about it is that the part of the picture which represents a picture is by no means well painted."

Forbera's painted cut-out seems to have been made for Louis XIV. See G. de Loye, "Le trompe-l'œil de Fort-Bras," *Revue des Arts*, IX-X, 1960, p. 19.

[16] See Jacques Wilhelm, "Silhouettes and Trompe l'Œil Cut-Outs," *Art Quarterly*, 1953, p. 296.

[17] Bernard Palissy, quoted in Marcel Raymond (editor), *La Poésie française et le Maniérisme*, Geneva, 1971, p. 13.

[18] Roger Caillois in the catalogue of Christian Renonciat's exhibition *Sculptures*, Galerie Alain Blondel, Paris, December 1979.

Chapter 8 (page 96)

[1] Collier confirms once again his allegiance to a militant Protestant milieu. Melanchthon (1497-1560), German scholar and humanist, was Luther's collaborator and wrote the Augsburg Confession (1530).

[2] Lazzari's picture is the companion piece of another organized in the same manner. The same layout is taken over in two other companion pieces by Lazzari shown in the exhibition *Inganno & Realtà*, Galleria Lorenzelli, Bergamo, 1980 (Nos. XXVIII-XXIX).

[3] This view was put forward by Clotilde Misme, "Deux Boîtes à Perspective Hollandaises du XVIIᵉ," *Gazette des Beaux-Arts*, 1925, p. 156.

[4] The problem is discussed by H. Schwartz, "Vermeer and the Camera Obscura," *Pantheon*, III, 1966, p. 170.

[5] See K. G. Hultèn, "A Peep-show by Carel Fabritius," *Art Quarterly*, 1952, Vol. 15, p. 97.

[6] Quoted in Clotilde Misme, see note 3 above.

[7] Leonardo's anamorphosis of a child's head is in the *Codex Atlanticus*, 1483-1518, Biblioteca Ambrosiana, Milan. See Jurgis Baltrusaitis, *Anamorphoses*, Paris, 1969, p. 36.

[8] See J. Baltrusaitis, *Anamorphoses*, Paris, 1969, and G. Barrière, "Des objets peints non identifiables," *Connaissance des Arts*, 288, February 1976, p. 48.

The Fortune of Trompe-l'œil (page 102)

[1] E. H. Gombrich, *Art and Illusion, A Study in the Psychology of Pictorial Representation*, London, 1960, p. 53.

[2] For a historical study of trompe-l'œil, see Celestine Dars, *Images of Deception. The Art of Trompe-l'œil*, Oxford-New York, 1979.

[3] Marcel Raymond (editor), *La Poésie française et le Maniérisme*, Geneva, 1971.

[4] W. Draeger, "Trompe-l'œil," *Du*, Zürich, No. 472, 1980.

[5] For the interest of contemporary thinkers in trompe-l'œil and their interpretation of it, see J. Baudrillard, *Le trompe-l'œil*, Centro Internazionale di Semiotica e di Linguistica, Università di Urbino, 62, 1977, and P. Charpentrat in *Nouvelle Revue de Psychanalyse*, 4, 1974.

List of
Illustrations

Index

Book design and layout by
Sylvia Saudan-Skira

Text and colour plates printed by
Imprimeries Réunies S.A., Lausanne

Binding by
H.+J. Schumacher A.G., Schmitten (Fribourg)

Printed in Switzerland